G000146024

SPEAKING
from our
HEARTS

MASTERING THE GAME OF LIFE

Global Co-authors Share Their Inspiring Journeys of Transformation

Jenni Burridge · John Smith · Jephias Mundondo · Kevin Searcey

Cherri Forsyth · Colleen Williamson · Sam Adams · Neil Millard

John Batterby · Lucie Bradbury · Liz Brown · Lyn Smith

Frank Clark · Paul Hart · Matt Youdale · Bill Burridge

PAUL D. LOWE

R3THINK PRESS

First published in Great Britain 2017
by Rethink Press (www.rethinkpress.com)

© Copyright Paul D. Lowe

All rights reserved. No part of this publication may be reproduced, stored in or introduced into a retrieval system, or transmitted, in any form, or by any means (electronic, mechanical, photocopying, recording or otherwise) without the prior written permission of the publisher.

The right of Paul D. Lowe to be identified as the author of this work has been asserted by him in accordance with the Copyright, Designs and Patents Act 1988.

This book is sold subject to the condition that it shall not, by way of trade or otherwise, be lent, resold, hired out, or otherwise circulated without the publisher's prior consent in any form of binding or cover other than that in which it is published and without a similar condition including this condition being imposed on the subsequent purchaser.

Cover image © depositphotos.com / sun_tiger

Praise

I have known Paul for many years, since my days as a Headteacher. His drive, enthusiasm and positivity were inspirational then to me and to my students. His authenticity and insight have only grown from there and I am proud to endorse him here.

RICHARD GERVER
Best-selling author | Game-changing speaker | Broadcaster

As Paul's coach and mentor, I know the benefits of his 'Three Pillars of Life' model can be life-changing. Paul's journey – from pain to prosperity – has been achieved by 'letting go' and he now uses his passion and drive to positively change other people's lives, globally.

JIM BRITT
Mentor and coach to Tony Robbins for five years |
Business partner with Jim Rohn for ten years | Leader in
the personal development industry for forty years |
Over a million attendees in seminars

Nottinghamshire YMCA has been pleased to see the partnership with the HEARTS brand grow from strength to strength. Thanks to Paul's leadership, commitment and drive, our programmes have been able to support hundreds of disadvantaged young people to benefit from a variety of life-changing sporting and educational challenges.

WILL WAKEFIELD
CEO | Nottinghamshire YMCA

The Proporta Education Foundation is hugely grateful to Paul Lowe and HEARTS Global for their donations to our charity. This kind of generosity makes it possible for the students we support in Sri Lanka to continue with their studies and to go on to achieve success against a background of often heart-breaking poverty.

GUY MONSON
Director | Proporta, www.proporta.org

Paul has applied his skills very successfully in helping and mentoring many people to get their lives back on track following setbacks, and he recently provided mentoring classes in Nottingham for groups of young footballers at Notts County Football Club. The feedback that I have been given from those who attended is that Paul's message has been an inspiration to them and one that aspiring young footballers should follow if they wish to achieve their goals.

LES BRADD
Notts County Football Club Ambassador |
All-time record goal-scorer for the club

CONTENTS

PART THREE

YOUR PATH TO PROSPERITY

159

INTRODUCTION

This book has been put together with a two-fold purpose in mind. Firstly, to offer real-life stories, insights and messages which will hopefully serve to inspire you to want to be more and love more. Secondly – but equally important – is to then have the awareness that you are able to give more, make a difference and leave a positive legacy.

It's interesting to hear people's understanding of the word legacy; some are already very clear and driven towards achieving what it means to them, while others probably don't even realise they are contributing towards a legacy in some way every single day of their lives.

This thought-provoking contrast is encapsulated in a quote from Oprah Winfrey as she turned to her friend and mentor Maya Angelou, and stated, 'I was so proud of myself for building a school for girls in South Africa. That's going to be my greatest legacy – this school.' (Winfrey, 2017).

Maya replied with her sage words: 'You have no idea what your legacy will be. Your legacy is every single person who watched your show and said, "I am going to take better care of my health"; every mother who saw a show on abusing children and said, "I will never hit my child again". To be able to do that, that's your legacy; your legacy is every life you ever touch.'

Consider what the word legacy means to you. It is easy for you to become an Ace of HEARTS (HEARTS being an acronym for Helping Everyone Achieve Results Towards Success); it's simply about raising your awareness.

Just as your own understanding of your legacy will be subjective, so too will your individual perception be of two other key words in this book – pain and prosperity. In very simple terms, pain for me has become a positive lever to gain the awareness to change, while prosperity means living a fulfilling life.

My own account in Part One, 'Emerging From The Forest', is comprehensively supported by Part Two which features contributions from co-authors from around the globe, with each one offering their own inspirational journey of transformation. I have consciously chosen a diverse array of friends and colleagues so that a rich mixture of messages may be conveyed. This may also be a platform for you if you have your own story or message to deliver to the world, as it is my vision to add more books to this series.

The third and final part of the book, 'Your Path To Prosperity', focuses upon some steps you can take next to live a fulfilling life, touching upon key considerations like your purpose, identity, vision and values. This is part of my legacy – using my experience to be a coach and mentor to others.

Throughout the book, the inspirational chapters are enhanced by simple one- or two-liner Words Of Wisdom (WOWs) along the way.

WOW

You cannot change what you aren't aware of –
awareness is a solid foundation for growth.

Leave past pain behind
and change to the path of prosperity

PaulLowe**HEARTS**

PART ONE

From Pain To Prosperity

PaulLowe**HEARTS**

Emerging From The Forest

PAUL LOWE
(UK and Spain)

Although now enjoying a life of prosperity, split between the UK and Spain, I spent most of my life living in Nottingham, England, embroiled for decades in an existence of deep-rooted emotional pain and suffering, fuelled by a volatile cocktail of alcohol addiction and violence.

During my colourful journey – dominated by a polarised black or white approach to life – I had a strong urge to write a book, and so in 2000, I self-published *The Game of Life: Half-Time Reflections*. This was an autobiographical account of my challenging journey during the first four decades of my life.

Although I now perceive it to have been badly written, people still feed back that it's a 'good book' and well worth the five pound investment I charged at the time. My cringe-factor is alleviated somewhat by the fact it made me three thousand pounds in profit – not bad for someone who took a risk and didn't really know what he was doing.

> ## WOW
>
> Be prepared to try different things – it's amazing
> what growth there is in embracing something new.

As I contemplate the colourful picture my life has unfolded to produce, I believe it has been one 'L' of a journey! After my parents split up when I was three, my mother and I moved to an inner-city council area called Bestwood Estate to live with my grandmother, Winnie. We were soon joined by a beautiful mongrel called Rocky – boy, how I loved that dog!

Although we were extremely poor, I recall fond memories of those impoverished days – until the age of about seven, that is. That's when my mother started seeing a man who lived next door to us, and a year later, in 1968, she married him.

As much as I look back on the first eight years of my life with pride and happiness – nostalgically reflecting upon a golden era of indulging my passions for music and football – I'm polarised in my recollections because my new stepfather's despicable, destructive and depraved behaviour changed my life for the worse. Starting out with random acts of abuse, neglect and mental cruelty towards my mother and me, he progressed on to consistent spates of sickening violence towards us both. This beast knew no bounds to his levels of cowardly, grotesque actions.

WOW

Let go of the pain from the past,
but not the lessons learnt.

As a result of this marriage, we uprooted from my beloved Bestwood and moved to the other side of Nottingham – to the countryside. For a city boy like me, it was a living hell. All the love and security I had ever known was removed from my world and I felt so desperate and sad. My certainty had been taken away from me – contact with my grandma, Winnie; my passion for listening to music; and above all, the dream that maybe one day I would become a Nottingham Forest player. My whole existence had become an unstable mess almost overnight. The country-boy kids didn't like football, and the beast deliberately deprived me of the two fervent passions in my life.

This acute loss lasted for two long, distressing years until my exile was temporarily over. I can still recall the elation – at the tender age of almost ten – when my mother told me she was leaving him.

In September 1970, I returned for the final year to my old Junior School and passed my 11+ exam, which gained me a place at the nearby Grammar School. I was now back home and free to enjoy my music and Forest; life was blissfully good once again.

However, this euphoria turned out to be short-lived on several counts. Firstly, I had begun to feel insecure and depressed because of the cruelty my mother and I had suffered from the beast; this scarred me more badly than I had realised, and the negative legacy was to live on for years.

Secondly, football was banned from the Grammar School. It was steeped in a tradition of playing rugby, and any mention of football was frowned upon by the (mostly) Victorian-style masters presiding over us.

However, if these two aspects caused me distress, they were nothing compared to what transpired later. Within a few weeks, my mother was reunited with the beast, and once again, my world was shattered. This marked the start of another three torturous years.

All his promises of change and happiness soon disappeared and the violence and heartlessness returned with a vengeance – and all this when I was still barely eleven years old. I tried running away from home a couple of times and nervously slept rough on the nearby common. My only salvation through this living hell was the fervent belief that I would one day be playing for my beloved football club, Forest, but this obsession was gradually being challenged by a new-found coping mechanism – the demon drink.

My mother was a secret drinker, and by the age of twelve, I was regularly helping myself to tots from her stashes of sherry and whisky. I became addicted. I was at breaking point and my ever-growing instincts for survival were being tested to the limit. By now, the cruelty and violence I was experiencing at the hands of the beast were having a dramatic knock-on effect on me, compounded by witnessing my mother regularly taking beatings from him.

In March 1974, after significant back-to-back defeats for my beloved football team, I realised that the demon drink was unable to sufficiently numb the effects of my physical, mental and emotional pain and I attempted suicide.

This was one of those 'fight-or-flight' moments, and I made a decision never to flee again. I somehow had the faith to accept there was a reason for this test. If I was experiencing this heartache, surely others would be too, and I was prepared to fight for them as well, consciously accepting my life now had purpose.

> ## WOW
>
> A decision to change your life
> can be made in an instant.

Such was my anguish at home that I was now creating a diversionary tactic: I was developing another character, one that would allow me to escape and become somebody else; a facade that was perceived by others as me being a no-nonsense hard-nut, not caring about anyone or anything. By the time I was barely sixteen, my passion for music was becoming irrelevant, and being replaced by the call to fight for others. This, along with my love for Forest, gave me a strong sense of identity and purpose. My passion towards Forest was beyond most people's comprehension, even many die-hard red-shirt supporters.

Looking back, I believe this extreme passion was a manifestation of an all-or-nothing mindset. There was no in-between. Forest gave me an identity at a time when I had effectively lost my own.

WOW

Your identity is not about your history,
it's about what you create for yourself.

By now, I found myself strongly drawn towards the Irish fraternities, regularly visiting the allotments (caves) of the men-folk on Sunday mornings for a nip or two of potcheen (home-made Irish potato wine) and tales of bare-knuckle fighting. Although I was naturally a loving, caring and sensitive type of child, I had developed a safety mechanism that kept people at arm's length. This front was displayed by an aggressive and confrontational persona – in effect, I was living a massive lie.

In November 1974, things came to a head and changed me for ever. After being kept behind at school for a detention, I knew that returning home late that afternoon would mean big trouble. I was trembling with anticipation as I sprinted home with the nervous energy of a hunted gazelle.

As I entered the back door, the inevitable happened: the beast attacked me mercilessly. I somehow weathered the onslaught and wiped the streams of crimson blood from my face. As I did so, I caught sight of a bread knife on the kitchen table. I lunged for it and took my stance with only one thought in mind, and it wasn't to cut bread. The hunted had become the hunter. My temper was so fierce, like that of a caged and tormented tiger.

This was the first time I became conscious of my ability to take control of my life away from the beast. Like all bullies when threatened with their own treatment, he cowered away.

The anticipated brutal escalation having not materialised, my mother and I simply packed our bags and left, with me vowing to the beast that one day I would return and get my revenge.

This proved to be a significant turning point in my life. Because of all the emotional pain I had suffered over the previous few years, I now found myself more alcohol dependent than ever, at the same time becoming embroiled in constant conflict and fights. As I progressed beyond my teens, one of the lowest points of my life occurred on New Year's Eve 1982 with the news that my grandma Winnie had died. As an 'old-school' matriarch, she had been so resilient, strong, and was as solid and tough as a majestic oak tree.

After Winnie's death, to say I waged war on society would be a massive understatement. I took it upon myself to be judge, jury, and executioner towards any Tom, Dick, or Harry whom I perceived to be a bully. I was now a rebel with a cause.

For a while, though, sheer willpower and determination saw me turn things around. At the age of twenty-three, I got married, and by twenty-seven I had two beautiful children and a third on the way. However, the cracks reappeared as I'd never managed to consistently curb my drinking – the demon drink had me in its vice-like clutches.

In June 1988, some fourteen years on from my suicide attempt, I reached rock-bottom in my life. I split up from my wife and kids and began to drift into complete oblivion. Like those of all heavy drinkers, my thought processes had become badly distorted and I couldn't rid myself of the memories relating to the previous torture and abuse. I constantly relived every slap, punch, and sadistic act the beast had delivered to my mother and me.

It was at this point that I finally confronted the beast. All the years of hatred had been allowed to fester, and in my emotionally-twisted logic, it was now time to redress the balance for all the anguish and pain he'd caused. The upshot was that I saw it as my duty to kill him, but the universe intervened with both our lives being spared – his from death and mine from serving a life sentence in prison.

WOW

Learn to control your thoughts
or else they'll control you.

Coming so close to totally ruining my life instigated another 'dry run'. I was reunited with my family, I got a good job and was starting to do what I'd been put on this earth to do – help others. However, my significant fundraising exploits would always be tested by heavy drinking binges.

Subsequently becoming unemployed in 1991, I decided to embark upon a long phase of learning – spanning over a decade – that resulted in me achieving a Teaching Degree and a Master's Degree. My studies fitted in around disciplined periods of abstinence, before I inevitably reverted to wild benders.

More important than the academic achievement was the process of continuous improvement that resonated with me. In retrospect, this philosophy was instrumental in laying the foundations for my personal development journey. I was greatly inspired by the prospect of becoming the best I could be, and then serving others.

WOW

The greatest investment you can make
is in yourself. If you don't believe in you,
how will anyone else?

While this was an admirable focus, I was still dealing with my own demons. My views were very polarised – life was either black or white, and I rarely showed any flexibility, especially in matters of potential conflict.

Irrespective of this, I look back over the decades and reflect on what lessons I have learnt and how these can be passed on for the benefit of others. Lessons not in an academic sense, but in a real, practical, life-improving sense. Put simply, I don't want people to learn the hard way like I did.

The breakthrough in my constant progress-sabotage cycle appeared after an almighty binging session. On 7 February 2010, I barely awoke from a drunken stupor. I thought I was going to die; I believed my time had come.

Throughout the following critical days, I somehow mustered the awareness that life would have to be very different if I survived. Obviously, I did, and to this day, I haven't touched a drop of alcohol since then.

One of my founding beliefs had been that the only way out of the hard-fought days in Bestwood would be sport or education. After spending so many years believing sport was the answer, I find it ironic that education and learning proved to be my salvation.

A by-product of my education was a poem about the demon drink.

A Question of Bottle

A man in his prison cell, all alone and he's down;
His eyes are all bloodshot and his face wears a frown.

One way or another, a life behind bars.
He once had it all, fast money – fast cars.

But now he is broken and everything is lost;
The legacy of booze, was it all worth the cost?

He needed his tipple to help him get by.
Now everything's gone, he wished he'd stayed dry.

The drink was a comfort when things got too tough;
At night he felt numb, in the morning just rough.

The lies and the violence he promised would cease,
But booze had control and never gave peace.

Tears stroke his cheeks as he thinks of it now.
Perhaps he would change, if only he knew how?

It's a question of bottle and which one to choose:
The one full of love or the one full of booze.

Neither is easy and both promise gains,
But one offers hope – the other just pains.

So, when you're alone with only booze as your friend,
Reach out for support – it's easier in the end.

Even in my darkest hours, I had a sense of purpose – albeit vague – that has continued to grow over the decades. Today, my awareness manifests itself in the work I do both as a coach and mentor, and also through the charity and community projects I'm involved in – embracing my identity as The HEARTS & Minds Mentor. All my life, I've committed to making a positive difference in others' lives, never more so than since the formation of the HEARTS community-enhancing entities and offering global support with local benefits.

I now recognise that all those years in the 'dark soil' were merely part of a planting exercise for when the environmental conditions were right for this particular acorn to transform into a thriving oak tree, making significant contributions to life's universal forests.

I stopped living a lie and reclaimed my true identity of being a loving, caring and sensitive man. I have come to understand the importance of love – for myself and others – as the emotional water in life's deserts. I know the benefits and positive impact of constantly striving to meet your needs for growth and contribution.

Imagine what my life would have been like if the pieces of my jigsaw had contributed towards creating a completely different picture. Can you imagine what my life would have been like if my mother hadn't married the beast in August 1968? As a result, I wouldn't have endured long-term pain and suffering, which forged my vision to leave the world a better place. What might my life have been like if:

- I hadn't made that suicidal fight or flight decision in March 1974, vowing never to become a victim again, instead committing to a lifetime journey of **Learning**?

- In September 1991, I hadn't made the decision to discover self-awareness and the importance of relationships and **Loving**?

- In October 2010, I hadn't formed the Sporting HEARTS charity and latterly HEARTS Global, positively affecting thousands of lives and leaving a global **Legacy**?

Although your past cannot be changed, it will contain some colourful pieces that can be used to create a new, more empowering picture for your life. I did just that with my 'Three Pillars of Life' approach.

At the beginning of this story, I alluded to my life being one 'L' of a journey. The reality is, it can be summed up in its entirety – as I believe life can for each and every one of us – by the 3L's: **Learning**, **Loving** and **Legacy**.

WOW

Leave your legacy in people's hearts,
then it's indelible.

Take one small step forward each day.
Remember, it only takes a few simple seeds
to grow a densely populated forest

PaulLowe**HEARTS**

PART TWO

Global Contributions

PaulLowe**HEARTS**

From Hell To Healing

CHERRI FORSYTH
(South Africa)

Our lives were irrevocably changed on 17 February 2002 when our younger daughter Kerry died, aged nine. She died following an operation to remove a non-malignant tumour from her pituitary gland. When the doctor told us she was brain dead, I just remember grabbing his hand with a long moan of *Nooooo!*

We left the hospital numbly that morning, with achingly empty arms, and returned to a home without our Kerry – our 'bubble of joy and enthusiasm'. Previously our home had been alive with the sounds of her excited chatter, and now we were plunged into a hollow silence.

I woke up every day for many months afterwards feeling that I had experienced a terrible nightmare – consistently thinking, *Oh, how awful, I know it will go away when I wake up*, only to find it crushingly true. It felt like part of me had been ripped away.

I now had to adjust to a new 'normal' with my husband Mike and older daughter Cathleen. Words don't even come close to describing how I felt – shattered into a million little bits; bleak, heavy and overwhelmed with waves of excruciating pain at the thought of living the rest of my life without her – physical pain in my heart. And how I cried and cried. I didn't know there could be so many tears in one person. The raw pain, longing, pining, missing were all too much. I felt my sobs coming from deep within my gut, fuelling moans of anguish. I just couldn't stop them…they came, and came, and came.

Initially there was a lot of care from our community, but gradually – as is to be expected – it dried up. By this time, my husband Mike was also unable to speak about the loss of Kerry. I felt isolated and surrounded by a dark swirl of pain and loneliness, shunned by others. It was like I had become someone else because of the loss of our daughter; people who used to greet me now suddenly pretended they didn't know me. Adding to the pain of our loss, we sadly lost relationships with dear friends and family – pain on top of pain. I can only think that they thought losing a child was contagious, or that they wanted us to be the same people we were before Kerry died – which was obviously impossible. How could anyone be the same after so much suffering, dealing with such fracturing grief?

About three months after the death of Kerry, I noticed a change in Mike. He was suddenly very angry and volatile. It started off with an incident once a month, then became once a week, until eventually it was many times a week. The only person who could really understand the loss of Kerry was my fellow parent, my fellow sufferer, my husband, and yet he cut himself off completely. In his place was a man who regularly shouted at me, blamed me for everything, was frighteningly irrational in arguments, always had to be right and accused me of all sorts of things. He was a complete stranger – where was the old Mike I loved? Where was my empathiser, my beloved husband?

Imagine my incredulity – a kind, loving, peaceful man had transformed into an abusive, cold monster. However, he reserved his appalling behaviour for me – outwardly he was as charming as ever, and he paid lip-service to psychologists so they thought he was dealing well with the death. Now in addition to my own grief, I was dealing with a stranger in our marriage.

As I fought to save our marriage, I was confronted with more and more bizarre behaviour from Mike, which made me wonder if I was losing my mind. I particularly recall after an all-night fight between us, he whistled off to work the next day, leaving me in a miserable huddle on our veranda, sobbing as I watched him go.

When he came home that night, I mentioned that we needed to resolve the issue from our fight.

'Which fight?' he asked, and when I replied, 'The all-night one,' he said that it hadn't happened. His behaviour was so awful that he couldn't even admit to it to himself. If he admitted to it, he would have to do something about it, and he didn't have the capacity to engage with his Monster Man side.

My husband was totally fractured, and I feared for his mental health. Another worry was added to my already over-burdened shoulders, while he seemed to have no worries at all in the world. But his eyes betrayed him – they were dead at their core.

As our marriage deteriorated, he became even more volatile. He then took to ignoring me. It was as if I didn't exist; as if I wasn't living in the same house as him. On one occasion, I was expecting him to take me to hospital for a minor day surgery – he forgot, so I drove myself. When he came home and I had a plaster over my nose, he pretended he didn't see it. He didn't ask me how I was, let alone apologise for forgetting.

Being ignored was telling me that I was worthless; not important enough for his attention; a nothing. It was one of the cruellest things he could have done. From feeling like a treasured, loved and worthy wife, I had been demoted to an invisible being.

I still battled on, fighting for a marriage I didn't even know if I wanted any more, and every step of the way I was being thwarted by Mike. This battle continued for eight years, with our marriage heading further and further into dysfunction. I was exhausted to my core, and bewildered. I had put my own grief journey on hold in order to put my emotional energy into caring for Mike and then trying to save our marriage, and yet all I received was abuse, blame, accusations.

I fought so hard because I knew this Monster Man was the result of Mike not dealing appropriately with the loss of Kerry, and that once he allowed himself to grieve, he would start healing. Then hopefully our marriage could recover. During all of these eight years, I never gave up hope – I always believed it would come right.

However, in 2010 – the year we both turned fifty and Cathleen turned twenty-one – he had an affair. The pain of this betrayal was the last straw to me. I finally lost all hope. A year which should have been filled with celebration was filled with barren-ness, pain, anger, rejection and disbelief.

Our teetering marriage was now absolutely shattered – there was nothing left any more. I really didn't care about him, our marriage, myself. I was in an emotional vacuum, which was my brain protecting me from the pain of the awful situation which had manifested. Having fought so hard to save the marriage I had treasured, I now crumbled, collapsed, and my heart shattered into bits I felt I could never put together again. I wasn't sure I could recover from this. I had lost a daughter, some friends, some family members, but I had valued my relationship and marriage above all other things, and now this too had collapsed.

What was left of me now? How much pain was I to endure? It was as if I had been flattened time after time by a ten-ton truck, and just as I was standing up, the next truck would arrive and flatten me again, and again, and again. Eventually it took me longer and longer to gather my resources and stand up between the aftershocks. Maybe it would just be easier to remain lying on the ground, then I wouldn't have to invest all my energy in getting up. If I just lay there, I wouldn't have very far to fall each time.

I requested that Mike leave our family home when I found out about his affair. My life was grey, without hope, without laughter. Just an endless nothingness – nothing to excite me; nothing to look forward to; nothing to live for; nothing…nothing…

Nothing?

Looking back, I realise how scary it was for me to feel nothing – I am sensitive and always care and feel so much, but suddenly the Sahara Desert had nothing on me. I was in a barren, heavy, dark, imbalanced and very unhappy place.

Gradually, though, I could see the darkness begin to lift and let the light in.

My rays of sunshine were our daughter Cath, my parents and sister, my sister-in-law, a few friends and my work as a Life Coach. Other than that, life was totally meaningless to me, so now came a time of profound introspection. What had this journey taught me? What was life all about? What was important to me? Could I teach myself to care again? Could I teach myself to be passionate about anything again? Could I ever laugh again? Where was I heading to now?

I started to put myself back together – slowly. I took a few months off work and was gentle with myself, spending many hours reading and growing in knowledge; doing anything to soothe my jangling soul; finding my mojo. I began exercising again, spending time with my family and trusted friends, but mainly I was pondering and thinking and pondering some more, always while listening to beautiful music.

Then I woke up one day with a flutter of excitement in my heart, albeit short-lived, and I knew that I was healing and would be OK. I had found out what my priorities were; I had found out who I was, my values, what I was prepared to put up with (or not) and what kind of life I wanted to live – with or without Mike. I realised I had overcome one of my greatest fears – the fear of being on my own. I could be happy on my own – I was a strong, independent woman. The steel core inside me had bent, but it didn't break.

So what happened to Mike, and our marriage? Well, Mike got seriously ill (and remains so until today) with a chronic and rare autoimmune disease, as well as diabetes. This was caused by stress – the stress of living a lie; trying to pretend that everything was fine, that he was coping well with the loss of Kerry. He finally underwent a powerful awakening, became conscious and experienced a metamorphosis. It was almost as if he had been living in a mist of fantasy, and now, as the veil fell from his eyes, he could see who he had become, the damage and hurt he had caused, the trust he had shattered – all the things of value that he had thrown away.

He started on a major programme of personal development, and slowly and painfully, a different man emerged. He became conscious, achingly aware of how he had been living since Kerry had died. He allowed the thoughts he had been blocking to flood his soul.

In doing so, he became aware of all the things Monster Man had destroyed. He could no longer deny them. Courageously he looked at the very worst of himself, didn't like what he saw, and worked hard to change it.

When I saw Mike putting effort into himself and our marriage, gradually my injured heart warmed a little to him. I had never stopped loving him, but I was still guarding my heart – it had been stomped on too many times. However, I started entertaining the thought of being with him again.

After a six-month separation, we got back together. We have both worked very hard to rebuild our marriage, using the hardship to weather ourselves and our marriage into something even more beautiful than it was before. We have both become strong individually, and hence together we are even stronger. We meditate together every morning, both work from home, take time each day to enjoy life and each other, socialise, and live a life filled with hard-won peace.

We now have a marriage characterised by love, laughter, authenticity, honesty, kindness, joy and connection. We will be celebrating twenty-nine years of marriage in September 2017.

WOW

The power of perseverance –
never give up on something you truly believe in.

No matter how long and dark the path is, there will always be some light at the end

PaulLowe**HEARTS**

Lucky Jim And His Guitar

FRANK CLARK
(UK)

I was born and bred in County Durham, around eight miles from Newcastle in the north-east of England. My father was a hardworking coal miner, and as an only child, I fondly remember my early years. My overriding recollection is of enjoying a warm, loving and secure upbringing. Although I don't think I was ever told by either of my parents how much they loved me, their actions reinforced that I was.

As was the way in those days in industrial communities, families in County Durham were very tight-knit, and mine was no different. Once again, I recall my extended family showing lots of love and support to me within a sports-oriented background – my dad was a good golfer.

As I reflect back upon my life and how lucky I've been, I often think about the timeless 'nature v nurture' debate, such as how a naturally gifted Northern Irish football player like George Best would have turned out if he hadn't been nurtured and heavily influenced by the football-crazy Belfast communities. I suppose the message is, talent alone is not enough – it needs to be supplemented with a strong work ethic and a healthy mindset. However, I was grateful for nature being kind and giving me a height of 6 foot 1 inch combined with 12 stone 2 pounds of weight.

Having enjoyed the immense benefits of being raised in a secure and loving family, I received my first awareness of pain – both physical and emotional – when I was twenty. I was playing for Crook Town Football Club at the time and had every intention of going on to university after completing my A-levels. However, fate had other plans for me. My A-level results were not good enough to get me a place at university and this disappointment lingered with me for a while, causing me some short-term emotional discomfort. I wasn't used to things not turning out as I had planned, so this was a big lesson learnt for me – that's life, deal with it!

I subsequently signed as a professional footballer for Newcastle United Football Club (NUFC) and my emotional challenge was soon to be followed by a more physical one – I broke my leg. Treatment for footballers in those days was sparse – there's only so much you can do with a bucket of cold water and a sponge – and so I was out of action for eleven months.

The big question at the back of my mind was 'Can I bounce back from this?' This temporary uncertainty was compounded by the death of my dad. On the back of these major challenges in a relatively short space of time, I consciously took the lessons from them and moved on as best I could.

As a professional footballer, I was having to distance myself from my old friends. My new-found focus as an athlete meant I had become far more aware of what was important to me, and to continue to grow,

I would need to leave some people and things from the past behind. This necessary detached approach was helped significantly by the fact that I spent some time in the NUFC reserve team – a lonely place to be at times. With all due respect to most of the old pros who accompanied me in the reserves, they were not the most inspiring role models; they were at the end of their careers and I had barely even started mine. Undeterred, I had the mindset to use this to my advantage; rather than dwell on my (temporary) misfortune, I used it as leverage to inspire and drive me on to bigger and better things. I would not become a victim of self-pity.

When I broke my leg, I was on the verge of breaking into the first team at NUFC. At the time, a player called George Dalton played the old-fashioned wing-half position, but the team manager – Joe Harvey – converted George to a left back, which was my key position too. One month later, George got injured and I got my chance. I played the last two games of the 1963–64 season, and from that point onwards, I was never out of the team for the following eleven years – quite a contrast to the squad rotation policy that seems to be favoured by a lot of modern-day managers.

To say life was prosperous would be an understatement akin to asking if the sun is a bit hot. The Dolce Vita nightclub in Newcastle became my haven – life was truly blissful, compounded by winning the Fairs Cup with NUFC in June 1969, beating Hungarian side Újpest Dózsa 6–2 over two games.

Shortly after that, I met my wife Pamela when I was twenty-seven. Historically, football managers have encouraged young players to settle down with a wife, rationalising that the responsibility of family life is far more conducive to stabilising players' careers than living the high life of a single man, and Joe Harvey was certainly no different. Interestingly, though, initially there was role reversal here: I provided Pam with the stability she needed because she'd had a challenging time while growing up. However, this 'investment' from me into a wonderful person like Pam would be paid back multi-fold in future years.

The 1974–75 season was my last at NUFC. Left-back Alan Kennedy was starting to challenge me for my Number 3 shirt and I intuitively felt that this was probably the beginning of the end, enhanced by an opportunity to go to America and become part of the ever-growing soccer revolution there. Not one to give in though, I approached Joe and sought reassurances about my future.

Joe set up a meeting with the chairman Lord Westwood, the latter categorically asserting, 'You're going nowhere!'

On the strength of this, Pam and I invested in a new house. However, this assured security was to be extremely short-lived. A matter of weeks later, I was given a free transfer. Looking back, I suppose that was my first introduction to the cliché 'There's no sentiment in football'. Once again, I found myself needing to change things, which was not helped by my missing out on the previous opportunity to go to America.

Within no time at all, I received an unflattering invitation to join the renowned manager Brian Clough at Nottingham Forest Football Club (NFFC): 'I'm desperate and need someone cheap – how you fixed?' This humble beginning was to become the start of a long association with NFFC as a player, manager, chairman and ambassador.

After spending four years as a player with Cloughie, I went to Sunderland AFC as assistant manager. I was there for two years before being sacked, paving the way for me to take the manager's role at Leyton Orient

Football Club (LOFC) for nine years, before returning to NFFC as manager between 1993–1996. The point of me highlighting these various moves is the approach I adopted to embrace one of the only certainties of life – uncertainty (change). My advice to anyone regarding this aspect of life is to accept whatever's happening and get on with it.

Always maintain a positive mindset and actively look out for new opportunities – welcoming change is one of the secrets to success, so be ready! I'm not saying it's easy, but it's certainly easier than allowing negative thoughts to take over and totally cloud and confuse the issue. The way I see it, it's a question of focus and not becoming distracted by external conditions that you have no control over. Ultimately, you are only responsible for your own actions.

This objective, laser-like focus is – I humbly believe – a trait of successful people. Indeed, Hylton Smith (an author from my native north-east of England) once described me as 'one of the most organised and tactical people I've ever known'.

The awareness of my internal thinking to handle the change process was certainly put to the test with a more external event that presented itself in 1995, the Bosman Ruling, which was to change the landscape of European football dramatically. More specifically, it added further constraints to the role of football manager. Within a month of leaving NFFC, I got the manager's job at Manchester City Football Club, but it was a huge relief when City sacked me.

Through all the stresses and strains that go with football management, I survived because of my own self-belief and one other vital factor – my family. Pam's influence in my life has been an immeasurable stabilising factor; while I was at LOFC, she was an absolute rock. She and our two beautiful daughters gave me reasons to stay strong, grounded and keep going, sometimes against all the odds.

While I pride myself on never taking the job home with me, I'm sure there were times when Pam saw through things, but she just maintained her strength and supported me anyway. My wonderful family is undoubtedly part of a great legacy.

This legacy also includes contributing towards making other people happy. Since retiring from football management at the age of fifty-five, I have come to realise the importance of everyday things like smiling at people and wishing them a good morning. It literally is the simple things in life that make a difference. I believe I've always been a good delegator, empowering people to work towards a clearly-communicated vision that is supported by the right mindset and values. As well as my own life legacy, I fervently believe I helped contribute towards strong positive legacies in football too – particularly at NUFC, LOFC and NFFC.

If I had to single out one person who has helped me create my football legacy, it would be a gentleman by the name of Bart Harwood. He was responsible for starting the under-elevens school football team I played in and igniting my passion for playing the 'Beautiful Game'.

The title of my story – Lucky Jim And His Guitar – reflects how fortunate I have been to have lived such a great life, with the guitar element embracing another key passion in my life – music. When I was around thirteen or fourteen, Lonnie Donegan burst on to the scene with his skiffle-style of music. This form of entertainment has been a great source of happiness and comfort in my life in good times and bad, and I particularly recall with fondness my own rendition of 'Worried Man Blues'. I've sung this song all over the world, making my 'singing debut' at the 100 Club in London's Oxford Street in 1997.

It is my sincere wish that you have managed to take some inspiration from my journey and I would like to close by offering two more insights:

WOW

The best team always wins, the rest is just gossip.
JIMMY SIRREL

Whatever focus in life inspires you,
always make sure you play with passion and desire.
We all have a message for the world - be heard!

PaulLoweHEARTS

The Power Of Pain

COLLEEN WILLIAMSON
(Canada)

Life offers many challenges, and pain can be an insurmountable part of the journey. The choices we make in any given moment will determine our path for the future. The choice is ours, and until we understand that we really do have the power within ourselves to create a better life, we may suffer as victims unnecessarily.

Do you ever find yourself asking, 'Why is this happening to me?'; 'Why can't my life just be different?'; 'Why do I have to live through so much pain around the challenges life has to offer?' Over the last couple of years, I have become keenly aware of patterns that ran consistently throughout my life, resulting from the choices that I made years ago. Recently, I discovered the impact of an early experience in my childhood and how I negatively interpreted its meaning into my own self-worth.

Growing up the youngest of four children, I was a shy and very emotional little girl. Being an 'Army Brat', I relocated with my family often, finally settling down in the city when I was the tender age of five. We moved into a little yellow house in a quiet crescent, a neighbourhood which I called home for the next ten years.

My secure childhood as I knew it was about to change. I remember sitting on my bed in an upstairs bedroom that I shared with my sister, and although I don't remember the exact words, the memory remains clear in my mind. My mom sat beside me as she gently explained what was about to change my life forever. Unknowingly, I would allow the divorce of my parents to affect how I made decisions for the rest of my life.

When we experience a traumatic situation, we make key decisions that help us rationalize what has just happened and why. Those key decisions become our subconscious survival mechanisms. Feelings of unworthiness, rejection and guilt that I had somehow caused my dad to leave our family were the meanings that I attached to that moment in my life.

This was a heavy burden for a young child to have to carry for so many years, although I recall some happy memories with both of my parents while I was growing up. Camping with my dad and his new family during the summer was a highlight; there was always something fun to do. I also remember crying when it was time to say goodbye, the pain resurfacing each time.

My parents were good, hardworking people, dealing with their own lives the best they could. My mom, often tired after a long day at work, would rest before supper. She seemed exhausted taking care of four kids while working full-time. Looking back, I realize that I may have tried to be the mother figure; being the emotional, caring type of person that I am, I must have sensed her struggle.

As we grew older, all four of us kids took our turns making dinner and doing household chores. I remember learning how to shop at a young age on my own. I would walk six blocks to shop for the groceries that were on the list for that week, fill out and pay by a cheque that my mom had provided, then take a taxi home. Mom did a good job of teaching us how to be responsible, how to cook and the value of a dollar. Interesting how two of us became chefs and one a baker.

I was popular and active, and participated in sports throughout my school years. It gave me the feeling of connection to people that I strived to have. Growing up, I spent a lot of time with my best friend; we lived close to each other and are good friends to this day. Junior High School started shifting things in my life. My friend and I would sneak out at night and we got into our share of trouble. We never did anything illegal; we were your typical rebellious teenagers.

My first heartbreak came in Junior High. I fell head over heels for a boy during the summer holidays, only to be rejected by him after I became pregnant. He was a year older and going onto High School. No matter how hard I tried to get his attention, he wanted nothing more to do with me.

The pain of that rejection took me years to get over. I was devastated and ashamed, wondering what I had done wrong. Ridden with guilt at becoming pregnant at such a young age, I made the most difficult decision of my life: to give away my baby boy. I felt unworthy of taking care of him, but somehow I was responsible enough to give him the chance at a better life than I was capable of providing. I had to believe in my heart that a life with two stable parents was the best for him, as devastating and painful as it was for me.

This, I have come to realize, is where I created the feelings of not wanting to be seen, not allowing myself to be heard, and burying my feelings deep inside of me, as it was such a lonely, uncertain and devastating time in my life. I always wondered what other people were saying about me, even though everyone in my life carried on as if nothing had happened. The fact that I had given away a child was never discussed. It was as if a part of me had died, but I was unable to grieve; I didn't know how to. I was ashamed and I held onto this pain for many years, never dealing with the loss of a child whom I have still not had the courage to try to find to this day.

Feeling the need to be in the company of my friends, I began to stay out past curfew. I wasn't trying to be a difficult teenager, I was just struggling to ease the pain of what had happened in my life; trying desperately to fit in again and regain some sort of a normal life. At times, it was awkward.

After a few months, my parents decided that it was best that I go live with my dad in a small town, two hours away. It had become too difficult for my mom to look after me as I was depressed and started missing school. I couldn't grasp anything. Learning was a challenge. But I was now at a point in my life where I really didn't want to move and leave my friends.

Starting High School in a small town was different. Everyone knew everybody else's business. I made a few friends and life continued. It wasn't long before I met a boy, two years older than me.

I began to stay out late and disobey the rules once again. Within a year, I had run away from home and moved several hours away with my new boyfriend. I dropped out of High School; it seemed as though following through with anything that would move me forward in life wasn't important enough. I wasn't worthy of making something of myself; I was always struggling, continually self-sabotaging any efforts for success throughout my life.

My relationship quickly became controlling. I felt alone and trapped in an abusive situation far away from anyone I knew. I was manipulated to stay with lies that he was dying. For nine years, I was convinced that I wouldn't amount to anything, so why should I even try? I felt stuck, frozen with fear, completely exhausted. I analysed everything to avoid starting an argument. Instead of wanting to be with people, now I began to isolate myself from everyone. Alcohol and drugs brought out the anger in him and the fear in me.

The feelings of shame crept in even more; I thought I must have done something to deserve this. 'I don't know what to do,' became a statement I repeated often while in distress, without realizing the impact it would have on my life. That statement affected who I was, and how I made decisions moving forward.

Looking back, I see its effects on my subconscious mind. I lacked confidence and clarity and have always had a difficult time making decisions, often procrastinating. Because I burned 'I don't know what to do' into my mind, it kept me stuck for years. I was numb to the pain of constant verbal, emotional and physical abuse; being lied to and cheated on. I distanced myself from my family as I felt ashamed that I had let them down. Was I really that bad a person? Why was this happening to me?

Despite several attempts to leave, I would invariably return to the familiar patterns of abuse. It took nine years until I finally became strong enough to break free, as difficult as it was. My confidence was beaten down and self-esteem was non-existent. I felt much older than my twenty-five years, but I intuitively knew I had to protect my two children from being affected any further. They had already seen too much. I was realizing that my life was not normal, and being a victim of domestic violence had to stop.

However, I have found myself in more dysfunctional long-term relationships since then, becoming involved with a new one immediately after ending the previous one. This never allowed me the chance to heal any part of my life as a person or become a better mom for my children. The relationships never felt truly fulfilling. It was as if I was trying to fill a void in my life. I couldn't commit to marriage; much like many things in my life, I found committing to something personally was difficult, although when I gave my word to an employer, I would give everything to the point of being a perfectionist and workaholic.

When I was thirty-five years old, my dad was diagnosed with cancer. I watched as he suffered; it was extremely hard for me to see him in such pain because he had always been a strong and disciplined man. The cancer took his life and he died of Multiple Myeloma. I became extremely depressed with no energy to function.

Losing my dad created immense sorrow in me that lasted for years. I remember asking myself, 'Why did he leave so soon?'; 'Did I cause him to die?'; 'Should it have been me?' as I felt I was the unworthy one. The grief of his death consumed me to the point that two years later, I was diagnosed with Stage 3 Non-Hodgkins Lymphoma, which soon turned into Stage 4. The treatment wasn't working, and now I had my own two-year battle for my life. I feared what would happen to my children; they needed me and I wasn't ready to die.

Pain is inevitable; long-term suffering is not. Emotional pain can control us if we allow it to. When we focus on what we don't want, we bring more of exactly that into our lives. Focusing on what's going wrong can become an addiction where we seek out people and events that will keep us in that familiar state. Even though we know we don't want that kind of life, we are almost certain it's going to happen, so we stay stuck in the cycle. Often people will stay in an unhealthy situation rather than risk moving into the unknown, even if the latter is a better option.

Overcoming the challenges and struggles in my life, I have become very aware of why things happened and what meanings I attached to the events of my past. I have come to realize the answer always lies within me, not from any external source or validation. Surviving cancer was a turning point in my life. Something inside of me woke up and I started a new journey of personal growth – one that continues to this day.

Over the years, I have immersed myself in personal development and spiritual growth, incorporating meditation, neuroplasticity and several healing modalities into my life. I have become certified in the Tony Robbins Coaching Program, and more recently a Trainer and Certified Coach in Brainsweep Systems, a powerful brain technique that has the ability to limit and relieve the effects of trauma in all areas of life. I have come to know that pain is an inevitable part of life. However, learning how to heal our emotional pain is something we must all do.

WOW

If sharing your own vulnerabilities can inspire one person, that can be the most powerful healing of all, and I believe the best legacy you can leave.

If you don't like the picture of your life - create some new images

PaulLowe**HEARTS**

Giving Youth
A Sporting Chance

PAUL HART
(UK)

I made my name in professional football as a centre-half, making my debut in 1970 for Stockport County. My playing career spanned eighteen years, and I amassed 567 appearances and scored forty-nine goals in the process. I began my management career at Chesterfield Football Club in 1988.

I was born in a place called Golborne – a mining village near Haydock Park Racecourse, England – and lived in a council house. My dad Johnny Hart used to travel to Manchester City Football Club's Maine Road ground – he was an inside-forward for City until he stopped playing in 1960 and became their manager. Only then, after Dad had purchased a house from the football club, did I really start to become aware of football, while also realising what a popular figure he was at Manchester City.

Although my brother Nigel – five years my junior – and I were both reared in a loving, stable family environment, we rarely got to see Dad in our earlier years. Mum finished work in 1953 once I had been born, and although times were hard – rationing was still around – we always had a full larder. As a family, we particularly understood the value of food.

From the age of around seven to eight, I slowly began to fall in love with football. Throughout the 1960's I progressed through my schools' football teams, and I vividly recall how Dad used to try everything he could to deter me from pursuing a career as a professional. He didn't think I was good enough.

At seventeen, I got my first professional contract at Stockport County. Dad regularly tore into me as a schoolboy, although I'm sure this chastisement was based upon some kind of management psychology and certainly for my own good, but once I'd signed professional forms, he was unswerving in his support for me.

As I enter my forty-seventh year in football, despite any inadequacies, I feel I've had a decent career, and certainly one that has provided me with a prosperous life. In terms of pain, this – like everything else in my life – is all in the context of football.

As a centre-half, I earned the obligatory 'designer nose' the hard way, along with my broken leg, but physical pain is something that comes and goes. At the age of thirty-five, I had to deal with a different kind of pain – finishing my playing career. I'd already gained my A-licence coaching badge, and in 1987, I was invited to go to Notts County as a player/coach. Following a year of cutting my 'coaching teeth', I then went to nearby Chesterfield Football Club as a manager. After getting the sack from there I went to Leeds United as Academy Director, employed by Howard Wilkinson, and it was there that I found my passion for youth football.

I realised I wanted to work with kids and use all the good principles I'd learned as a player. I'd worked under some really good managers, including a certain Brian Clough, and I was determined to pass positive traits such as good manners, having respect for referees and not feigning injury on to the young players under my charge. As a leader, I knew what I stood for and what I stood against, and things were not up for compromise. It was up to me to set the standards and ensure we all followed through on those standards, as Cloughie often used to say, 'From the Chairman to the tea-lady'. I believe creating a clear, positive culture is critical in any organisation if success is to be achieved.

Paul Lowe recently reminded me of something I'd said to him in 2000. I was the Academy Director at Nottingham Forest while Paul was working as part of the team delivering the education programme to the young apprentice footballers. At the end of the season, certain players would be released, and Paul said to me, 'It's that heart-breaking time of the year again, gaffer', my candid response being, 'Always remember, they'll leave this club as even better young men than they were when they first came here'.

The thing is, these young men knew that despite having to break the news that some wouldn't be kept on as professionals, we really cared about them. As mentors, we had a moral duty to make sure these boys felt valued and respected; they needed to know they mattered. In my opinion, this is a fact of life, not just in the world of football. For me, mentoring is about making positive changes bit by bit and continually practising the lessons learnt so they become embedded within people's lives and a way of being. By paying attention to the details, I know that a bigger, far more beneficial picture will emerge.

In 1978, I was Leeds United Football Club's record signing and I remember going through a challenging phase of my life. I can only liken it to being in a dark tunnel, probably due to the power of expectation and the fact that I wasn't playing very well. I don't know if I would describe it as depression, but I was unhappy and it was certainly a scary place to be. It's amazing at times like this how much your self-belief gets tested. I instinctively knew I had to work through this stark period and emerge from it victorious.

A low phase raised its head again once my playing career had finished. Being stripped of my sense of purpose, focus and routine – not to mention significance in life – was an extremely challenging ordeal to cope with. To compound this pain, I never really had a great sense of self-awareness then. This was epitomised by the fact that I never perceived myself to be a good player; I just responded to being given simple instructions.

These days, though, I realise the critical importance of self-awareness. I believe it to be the solid foundation from which everything else in life will progress and grow. It's futile to have regrets; we cannot change the past, only learn lessons from it, but sometimes I wish I'd been more sensitive towards other people. Forgiveness is something that I have generally struggled with. It takes a long time for me to forgive people, although I'm aware I've had more than my fair share of forgiveness from others. I'm also noticing these days that I'm becoming more resistant to change.

It is interesting, particularly in the world of football, how people learn to develop a façade. Mine was one of being a stern-faced, resolute character. However, many young people I have been involved in managing within football have seen my 'real' softer side. Having achieved successful goals in my life, not just in football, I reflect on what it will all have counted for. In other words, what will my legacy be? Ultimately, I'd like to think others will say, 'He's a good bloke.' That said, I firmly believe it's important to have self-validation rather than relying on external validation.

Part of my own moral compass is to constantly teach good values to others, and lead through example by committing to my own top five values of honesty, respect, humility, learning and development. My vision is simple: to inspire and influence people to become the very best they can be.

WOW

Always strive to create
your own legacy – be kind and caring.

If ever you find yourself going through a dark tunnel in life, have the Awareness to know what's happening; the Belief to know that you will emerge victorious and the Courage to endure the challenge – make it as simple as ABC!

PaulLowe**HEARTS**

Growing Pains

SAM ADAMS

(Spain)

Being born in the mid-sixties and raised in a small town in Dorset, I spent my early years in pain and suffering. My main challenges were around my race – having a black mother and a white father – and my sexuality, both of which combined to create massive confusion about my identity.

The only certainty I had in my life for many years was my own belief that I was some kind of 'freak'; that I was somehow a second-class citizen because of my skin colour. I even felt embarrassed of my mother because she was black. I hate even writing that now; I feel ashamed for thinking it, but the truth is that's what I thought as a mixed-up kid.

Because of how I felt about my colour and my mum, I didn't want my friends to come around. I just wanted to fit in and be liked. But I didn't – there were no other black kids in school except my sister and brother, and my brother had a really hard time of it. He certainly bore the brunt of the racism.

I always felt different walking into a room, and terribly self-conscious. Back then there weren't many black faces anywhere, very few on TV, and when it came to gay people – forget it! I heard racist and homophobic words all throughout my childhood – not necessarily directed at me, but they hurt and made me think I could never fit in. Back then, I couldn't go on the internet for support to try and understand my feelings; I just thought I would have to remain silent for ever and lead a fake life. I didn't dare tell anyone how I was feeling for fear that I would be ostracised.

It wasn't until I was in my early twenties, when I became depressed and got counselling, that I finally spoke to someone about my feelings. This was the start of a very different me. But it took years of unravelling, and to this day I invest heavily in myself to accept who I am. I undoubtedly owe a great deal to my parents for the life they gave me and the subsequent lessons they taught. But although my sister, brother and I were raised in a secure environment, our parents never told us or gave us hugs to show how much we were loved, the irony being they were loving towards each other. When I was in my thirties, I asked my mother why we were never shown any love – I was thirty-seven before I first heard her say she loved me, and my dad never has, to this day.

At the age of sixteen, I left home (due to the confusion around my race and sexuality) in a very angry state.

Agonisingly painful was the death of my brother-in-law, Tony, on 28 August 2005. He had been living in Anguilla and was only back in the UK for six weeks prior to his death. What compounded my pain was the fact he'd contracted Chicken Pox from my children. He was taking steroids for an eye infection, which seemed to weaken his immune system, thereby leaving him even more vulnerable to the virus. Tony and I were going to start a new property business together. I'd already sorted out funding, but this all turned out to be in vain due to these unfortunate set of circumstances.

What this whole excruciatingly painful experience served to do was to drive home the love between me and my sister, Yolanda. It brought us even closer together, along with my adorable little niece, who was only four months old at the time of her dad's death. They literally mean everything to me.

The other significant change that has happened since Tony's passing is how I've looked at life. I live in the here-and-now, grabbing every moment because I know from practical experience how life can be taken in an instant. Just as I'd previously created a mindset about being a freak, I have now exchanged it for one that is far more self-serving – the power of **now**.

Sharing my sister's pain has been life-changing. We're constantly asking ourselves, 'Did we spend enough time with Tony?' although this is a completely futile question because what's past is past. There is absolutely no point whatsoever in clinging to the distorted memories of the past – we can only learn lessons from it and move on.

It's interesting how people can misconstrue 'I need to put myself first in my life' as selfish, missing the point that I need to be the very best I can be. I need to take care of myself, then I can pass on any benefits to others. I liken it to having a safety briefing on a plane and being advised to put on your own oxygen mask before assisting others. This is a great metaphor for life – I'm sure we can all relate to giving something to others at the expense of our own well-being, be that time, love or money.

Money has been another 'pain lever' for me. Over a five-year period, I lost a total of £250,000 on various business-related initiatives. I cannot put into words the numbness I felt about this, especially as most of it was for my prosperity project to live my dream life in Spain. All the previous years' self-loathing, disgust and uncertainty raised their heads again – how could I have been so stupid? My own identity as a savvy businesswoman was shattered, compounded by the emotional leverage of knowing £100,000 of the money was my inheritance given to me in advance by my parents. In the absence of being able to rationalise it, I believed suicide was the only viable option. Looking back, I suppose my failed attempt was under-pinned by my awareness that I had been greed-driven.

I didn't tell my parents about losing their legacy money. I didn't feel it necessary to, but I did have a burning desire to finish my prosperity project off. There was only one small problem – I was now broke! Once again, money was the catalyst for a situation that, within the last three years, led to me leaving the house one morning vowing to myself I would not be returning. To this day, I still cannot remember what I did. It is a complete blank.

In a desperate attempt to recover my parents' legacy money, I borrowed £100,000, gambled the whole lot on Stock Trading, and lost. Once again, this was down to my own arrogance and greed.

Due diligence is one of the most painful lessons I've ever had to learn, while reinforcing the cliché of 'If it feels too good to be true, it probably is'. This certainly applies to me; it's something that I massively resonate with and endorse.

I suppose like most people, I wasn't overly aware of my potential legacy until I had the conversation with Paul. Why would I be? After all, the work I do as an Inspirational Speaker and Happiness Mentor is all about inspiring others in the here-and-now. The reality is, that's part of my legacy contribution to the world.

I've never felt as strong as I do now, but this doesn't stop me from continuously searching for new ways to grow and keep giving. I have learnt that it is so important to spend quality time with people – especially loved ones.

Pain is something that seems to be consistent in my life, but I am starting to understand that perception more positively, especially as I now live my dream life of prosperity in Spain along with my loving partner, Natalie.

I don't know if you have ever felt so low that the only way out seemed to be to end your life. As one who has had this life-challenging experience three times now, I can only plead with you **not** to take that option. You do have a light to shine on a world that's often in darkness.

WOW

Everything about what you think, say and do combines to create a totally unique light, known as your legacy. No one else will hold your torch, only you. Keep shining!

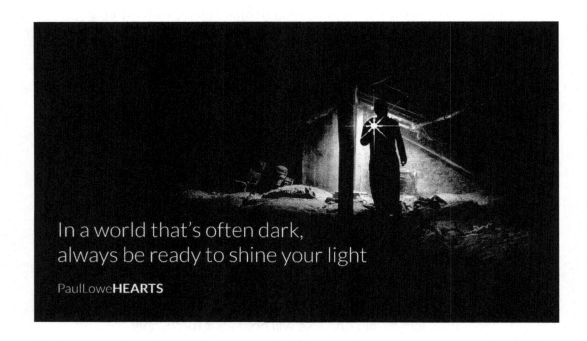

In a world that's often dark,
always be ready to shine your light

PaulLowe**HEARTS**

Sometimes It's For The Best

MATT YOUDALE
(UK)

Every so often in life, something significant happens over which you have no control. There I was in 2010, Director of Communications and Board member of a £1.2 billion National Health Service (NHS) organisation – thoroughly enjoying my well-paid executive role, overseeing a large team and making important decisions every day. Then the newly-elected coalition government began its controversial NHS reforms.

Six months later, I was out of a job, and the primary care trust I'd worked for was in the process of being wound up.

The shock was seismic. Yes, there was a redundancy package, but it wasn't big (I hadn't been in the NHS long enough for that). All sense of certainty and security had gone. More serious still was the sense of not being wanted, of being cast out. I tried to rationalise things and tell myself that I was just a victim of a politically-driven process, but the sense of rejection was unshakeable.

This was hard to take after a career in which I had become accustomed to success. During eighteen years at the British Broadcasting Corporation (BBC), I was lucky enough to win a fair few high-profile awards as a correspondent, documentary-maker and senior manager, before making the switch into corporate communications with the NHS.

Many people had asked me why I chose to leave behind the glamorous world of BBC journalism (at least, that was their perception of it). In the end, it had been a surprisingly straightforward decision. I had done lots of different things and was in danger of going stale. In covering some stories, I was getting a sense of déjà vu. I needed a fresh challenge.

In contemplating my future after redundancy, I returned to that same thought process. If I had been so keen to do something new when I joined the NHS in 2008, why should I worry about moving on again in 2011? With the benefit of hindsight, I can see that holding on to that idea was important. I avoided panic and focused on turning a challenge into an opportunity. I had to look forward, not back.

And so I decided to go into consultancy, swapping a regular job for the vagaries of the open market. Working for myself was something I had always wanted to try; there is something very appealing about the idea of being your own boss. The result was Arch Communications, a PR agency working on social enterprise principles committed to giving away at least 10% of profit each year to good causes.

Why do I do that? Quite simply, because I'm passionate about good business ethics. There is something wrong about the way big utility companies have lost the ability to treat individual customers as human beings, and global brands pay executives annual bonuses measured in the millions. How much money do these people need?

I was determined to do things the right way from day one – to give every client the same level of care, no matter how big or small they are. I always pay my bills on time, if not early. Never late. Nor do I shy away from doing someone a favour. This was something I brought from journalism, where my philosophy was that if I'm straight with people and show I can be trusted, I'm much more likely to get the story. I was proved right time and again.

Since we began trading in 2011, the company has invested more than £100,000 for social benefit through profit-sharing and *pro bono* work. We have focused on creating a legacy – helping charities, community groups and projects in the fields of domestic abuse, addiction rehabilitation, end-of-life care, volunteering, crime prevention, family cohesion and the environment. It is something in which I take great pride.

There is some commercial advantage to behaving in this way, although it is hard to quantify. It's certainly a talking pointing when I meet someone new. But more importantly, it says something about who I am and the way I and my business like to do things. Our PR work is all about reputation. This is a precious thing, and our reputation being closely associated with words like integrity and quality means a lot.

Setting up a company for the first time inevitably involves a steep learning curve – developing a business plan; acquiring a domain name and commissioning a website; grappling with spreadsheets and bookkeeping; doing VAT returns; realising just how long it can take to turn a business lead into paid work. And all at over the age of fifty.

I made plenty of mistakes. But that's part of the process, isn't it? In the early days, I was so keen to please potential clients that I offered up too much early on. I had to learn to demonstrate my expertise without giving people what they wanted free of charge. One good tip I was given was to offer discounts in return for testimonials (assuming the client was happy). This proved to be a useful way of building a work portfolio quickly.

Working out what to charge was especially tricky. It was tempting at the outset to set my prices too low because there wasn't much in the sales pipeline. But I quickly realised the importance of understanding the value of my knowledge.

Of course, it wasn't a total standing start. My knowledge of the media, love of writing and my strategic experience from the NHS were all valuable attributes in providing public relations support to others. However, I did discover to my surprise that some of my reporting skills and experience were directly transferable to the world of business. As a journalist, if I came across a hint of a story, I did the necessary research, reached out to people, established their trust, confirmed information, and eventually I had what I needed to publish or broadcast something. Some of the most satisfying things I worked on were those stories which were hardest to prove and which took months of hard graft.

In business, the process of turning a small lead into paid work is remarkably similar. It's all about engaging with people on the right terms, building relationships and being patient. This I could do.

After three years as an independent consultant, I reached another crossroads. I had become very busy and had a healthy income. But work occupied most evenings and weekends. There was no balance in my life, and I knew that the pace was unsustainable. Something had to give.

There was a straight choice. I could continue to fly solo and start saying no to offers of work – something I hate doing, because people rarely come back if you're not available the first time round. Alternatively, I could employ people and grow my company into something greater.

Because I still had ambition and wanted to be in a position to take on bigger clients and projects, I opted for growth. I have done this carefully, taking my time to find the right people and not over-extend the business. I have done quite a lot of recruiting in my time and I pride myself on making good appointments. Yes, the core skills matter, but for me it's all about culture. Will the person fit the team? Are they willing to learn? Do they have the right attitude?

One of the first people I took on was Ellen. She had a first-class degree in fine art from Lincoln University, but no meaningful PR training or experience. When we met for a chat, I knew within five minutes that I was going to offer her an internship. She had the necessary spark which showed me she was going to be good. And so it proved. The internship soon turned into a permanent job.

The same goes for the other people I have employed – I have trusted my instinct and it hasn't let me down. Today, as I write this, there are four others working alongside me and the company has substantial contracts. We are all different, but we make a strong, successful unit.

Being responsible for people adds complications, of course, and a whole new set of things to learn about – payroll, workplace pensions, training programmes, holiday entitlement... Having a bigger team means that I am able to delegate more, and I do have a much better work/life balance. But I am still on a hamster wheel. It is now simply a bigger wheel because I have more mouths to feed. However, the company is a more sustainable business and I have more time to dedicate to developing it further. Expansion was the right call.

Today, we are a well-established enterprise. Our clients range from large public organisations, like hospital trusts and local authorities, to global brands, start-up companies and small charities. We've won awards, including Silver for Outstanding Small Consultancy in the PR industry's regional awards. We're still growing and I'm starting to wonder whether our office is big enough. But there's no compla-cency. I still get moments when I'm lying in bed, wondering where the next job is coming from. That never leaves me. It could eat at me if I let it, but I prefer to use it as positive motivation, spurring me on to the next thing.

Those anxious days in 2011 now seem a long way away. Life is good. Yes, I have to work hard (sometimes at odd hours), but I have never shied away from that. I am my own boss and have the control to make my own decisions. In fact, I've probably become unemployable, since I cannot imagine being managed by someone else ever again.

I have a host of new skills and get enormous satisfaction from being told by grateful clients that I have done a great job. I also know that because I own the company, its success brings financial rewards. My ambition has been re-set. I started off merely aspiring as a one-man band to make enough to pay the bills. Now, I run a small business which I hope to grow and ultimately sell as a going concern.

It sounds pretty straightforward, doesn't it? But it certainly hasn't been. There have been plenty of dark periods when Arch Communications was losing money and I was filled with self-doubt. Throughout it all, though, I have had the great fortune to have unflinching support from my family. They were the ones who told me to 'go for it' and 'keep the faith'. There may have been trying moments in the early days when I was working off the dining room table and struggling to concentrate amidst the racket. But my wife and children have been a key part of my success.

As I sit and reflect today, I ask myself what the key learning points along the way have been. A few things come immediately to mind:

- **Never stop learning.** Anyone who stands still for too long in this fast-moving world is lost. You have to have the humility to want to continue to develop.

- **Live by your values.** Stick to what you believe in, and demonstrate that belief in the way you behave. It is important for others to understand who you really are.

- **Don't lose faith.** It is easy to lose heart and wave the white flag when things don't go according to plan, but no one succeeds by giving up.

- **Trust your instincts.** No matter how logically you try and approach things, sometimes you just have to believe in yourself and act on your own instincts.

- **Don't take things for granted.** Always be grateful for what you have and show that gratitude. Health, career and family all need working at. After all, if you take out without putting in, you will soon be overdrawn.

No two journeys are the same. Everyone is different. But the commitment to self-improvement and the importance of strong relationships are things which benefit us all. Through these, anyone has the capacity to succeed in life – and through that success to leave a powerful legacy.

WOW

A lesson in how mid-life redundancy
can be turned into a long-term positive

Beliefs - there's reality and then there are our own beliefs about what's real. Perhaps if things aren't working out, we need to change our own beliefs?

PaulLowe**HEARTS**

Taking Control And Rising Up

NEIL MILLARD
(UK)

I believe this chapter perfectly epitomises how much my head was in the metaphoric clouds – confusion abounding within my own personal world – and how this impinged massively on my ability to maximise my undoubted potential as an IT practitioner, compounded even further by a tale of extremes on my financial journey from bankruptcy to prosperity.

I was born to my parents David and Wendy in 1975. A year later, my little sister joined us. Another big change for our family that year was Dad joining the RAF, which meant lots of moving around, and before the age of nine I had already been lucky enough to live in Cyprus, Germany and the UK. In short, life was good.

When I was ten, my parents divorced and many things changed.

My mum moved my sister and me to the council estate where my grandmother's house was. Rather than an exciting life moving around the world, I was now confined to a small house in a brand new area with no immediate prospect of escape. I missed my dad terribly. In hindsight, I was lonely, but at the time I lost myself in computer programming.

At thirteen, I moved to Upper School and found acceptance with four fellow 'geeks' – a friendship circle that I still enjoy and am very grateful for today. This improved things for me and I started to gain an interest in girls.

I recently bumped into a girl I had really liked at school, and she said, 'I still can't fathom why you never asked me out.' My belief at the time, however, had me convinced that no girl would ever be interested in me. I became depressed, although to outsiders I must have seemed fine.

Another upheaval was imminent in the form of a move to live with my dad. There had been friction between Mum and me, resulting in a move just before my exams to Dad's caravan. I took my exams from there, and did well enough to get the grades for college.

I spent the summer holidays with Dad, then moved back in with Mum after tensions between my stepmother and me escalated, primarily owing to my desire to have my parents reunited and my misguided view that causing problems for my step-mum would somehow help this happen. Mum subsequently lost a lot of weight, remarried, and we no longer lived on a council estate. The family grew in the following years on both sides and I soon had three little sisters. I continued my studies at college, but the disruption meant I had missed the opportunity to go to university to become an aeronautical engineer. The Royal Navy had also turned me down because of my poor eyesight.

By 1993, I had achieved some A-levels and I was working in Cheddar Gorge as a seasonal worker, selling cheeses and cider. The money from the job meant independence; I bought a car and rented a room in a shared house.

Driving to work one day, I had a car accident. Once I had no car, I had no way of getting to the job, and I soon became unemployed. I went on welfare benefits for seven months, during which time my housemate helped me through a deal we struck where he'd buy the food and I would cook it.

Being on the dole (welfare benefits) meant I had time on my hands, and I used much of this to refine the programming skills that mean I can now work as a successful systems support consultant and run my own IT development business. I met some interesting characters along the way, one of whom introduced me to my now ex-wife, Janine. Many other positive things happened around that time, too – I got a new job with a water company, which included a car and meant I was able to ask Janine out and take her somewhere nice. On 25 July 1995, I collected my company car, started my new job as a trainee computer technician, and that evening took Janine for our first date. She even deemed the new me fit enough to marry, and a couple of years later we did just that.

We bought a house – heavily mortgaged. Having come from living off a mate in shared accommodation, I was now a proud homeowner and husband.

Janine quickly became pregnant with our first daughter, Melissa. Around twenty-five weeks into the pregnancy, we took a trip to visit Janine's brother. Janine began bleeding on the way and we spent our week's holiday in Crawley Hospital, where she had to have an emergency caesarean. Sadly, Melissa did not survive and we never got to meet her while she was alive.

What struck me the most at that tragic time was the huge loss of potential: who Melissa might have become; the things I could have taught her; experiences we might have had as a family. We held the funeral a week later then tried to get our lives back on an even keel. I returned to work and Janine became pregnant again. This time, Sophie was born two weeks early on 13 September 1999. It was a difficult pregnancy and another caesarean birth for Janine to endure, but our daughter was (and is) perfect.

Around the same time, I was offered redundancy and took it. The company that had forced the redundancy then recruited me at a higher salary. For the next four years, our family grew together. Janine and I enjoyed parenthood and family life, even with the occasional well-meant intervention from the in-laws.

Then I was offered redundancy again, this time without the immediate promise of another job. Although I was frustrated, it also meant I had more time to focus on a business I was trying to get off the ground. It never did, and financial troubles loomed.

I took contracting work, but our debts were still growing in spite of how hard we both worked and the sacrifices we made. This put immense strain on the marriage, and shortly after I moved permanently for the start of a new contract in Bristol, the relationship broke down altogether.

I moved in with one of my sisters; Janine and I divorced. I missed Sophie, but the divorce was the right decision for us and it felt like a fresh start. I remember getting some support from my mum, but it felt hollow somehow and I have since learnt to provide that support to and for myself.

The contract ended and nothing else was available. I was broke, divorced, missing my daughter and felt unemployable. I relied on the support of my friends and the occasional work contract, but my financial books still wouldn't balance – things seemed pretty hopeless.

Then I met a lovely lady called Wendy. With her love and encouragement, I finally settled into a permanent job with Sanctuary.

Wendy helped me to see a light at the end of the tunnel regarding my finances – I filed for bankruptcy and was really able to start afresh. Had I continued to strive to pay my debts off, I may never have done so and would probably have driven myself mad in the process. However, I was floored. The mind-shift to go bankrupt is huge, and I could only rationalise it by reminding myself that I'd actually paid off what I'd borrowed and only the interest remained. That softened the blow – a little.

The appointment with Cheltenham Court was two weeks after I'd originally plucked up the courage, paperwork and fees to go bankrupt. My job was still quite new, and I now had a steady income, plus a new relationship to enjoy. The budget advice from the CCCS (Consumer Credit Counselling Service) was helpful and I stuck to the budget for the required twelve months. But it was a tough year with very few treats. I was treated like a second-class citizen by most agencies: the council wanted their tax on a payment card; my mobile was pay as you go; the electric needs were paid on a key meter; rent had to be six months up front. I didn't dare even mention the word 'credit'. And I still got phone calls from people chasing the credit card debt. I referred these to the receiver, and the calls eventually subsided. It was cash payments for everything.

I was setting aside the money my budget allocated for new clothes, and started saving some cash up in a jar. The habit of keeping a cash buffer – what I like to call my self-funded overdraft – has stayed with me and I always carry at least £20 for emergencies.

By 2008, I'd created a financial cushion and was sticking to my CCCS budget plan even after the restrictions had been lifted. I got on with my day job and refined my budget so I felt comfortable and was getting back in control. A pay rise came in 2009, and I started spending again. This time, though, I reorganised my budget according to *my* priorities, not the government's. They're not too dissimilar, really, but when I was in the control of the courts, they didn't expect me to have the money or inclination to invest in savings, education, a safety net, or anything other than a pension.

I came across the work of T. Harv Eker. He introduced me to a concept of budgeting that resonated with me and formalised an idea I'd long held: that a budget is important and allocating money specifically to 'fun' will help protect the rest of it. The idea is that I can blow my fun money, not the amounts set aside to pay off essentials or for saving.

My learning about finance and my personal debt management continued at the same level while I worked at Sanctuary for the next five years, then there was another big leap forward when I attended a Broadband Consciousness seminar. This introduced me to a concept called The Script (a five-day discovery of who I actually was, rather than the man society and my parents had taught me to be). The Script gave me the confidence to look for contracts outside Sanctuary and begin developing my own business again. Two years on, I was running a business, moving from bankruptcy to business owner within seven years.

Throughout my life, I have experienced highs and lows. It has taken me a long time to come to terms with some of the events from my past and to use them positively. I owe much of this to my partner, Wendy, and two other very important influencers: firstly, being introduced to The Script, and secondly, to Paul Lowe for expanding my consciousness through his HEARTS Coaching programmes,

significantly helping me to discover and achieve my true life's purpose
— to grow, prosper and live a totally fulfilling and fun life. All-told, I
want to share this gift of new-found awareness and consciousness
with you to help on your journey.

WOW

If you're going through hell, keep going.
WINSTON CHURCHILL

Choices – you can either spend all your time on the ground
worrying about every blade of grass;
or you can rise up and conquer new fields

PaulLowe**HEARTS**

From Bridges And Ballet To Butterflies

BILL AND JENNI BURRIDGE
(South Africa)

'So, how do I look?' I asked Dave, my best mate and fellow engineering student at the University of Cape Town.

'Like a right tart,' he smirked.

'OK, give me another swig of that beer and let's go do this thing,' I responded, faking courage.

We were heading to a *Rocky Horror Show* themed party at the neighbouring ladies' residence. Dave's new partner, Gail, had pressed him to bring me along as a blind date for her friend and roommate, Jenni.

Picture the scene…beer-swilling engineering student in full cross-dress with borrowed stockings and skimpy lace underwear, attempting to impersonate Frank N. Furter.

As I think back to that defining moment in my life, I shake my head and laugh at my blissful ignorance of the universe's unfolding plan. I was about to meet the love of my life. What a first impression!

Mercifully, Jenni is blessed with a great sense of humour and our relationship continued, even after the 'rocky' start.

Amongst our peers in the engineering faculty, word spread quickly that Dave and I were dating students from the university's ballet school. Publicly, we revelled in the boost to our 'cool street cred'. Privately, however, we soon began to lament how under-equipped our calculator-and-logic type personalities were to deal with the emotional tempestuousness of our artistic-and-creative natured girlfriends. If you ever experimented with magnets and iron filings in a school science class, you'll appreciate the saying: 'Unlike poles attract'. Well, 'unlike poles' Jenni and I most certainly were. On reflection – Jenni and I have been married longer than Britney Spears has been alive – we may, ironically, have stumbled upon the secret to relationship longevity.

Post-university our relationship was soon put to the test. While I joined a major construction company specialising in bridge building and moved across the country, Jenni accepted an offer to run a dance school for kids and took off for the beautiful Indian Ocean island of Mauritius. After a year apart, I flew out, excited to join Jenni on a three-week holiday only to discover that she had begun to succumb to the charms of a softly spoken local man with an intoxicatingly romantic French accent. It was clearly an unfair competition and I had to act quickly. On the eve of Christmas at that symbolic turning point – sunset – I proposed.

Mother Nature, though, was not impressed. Within days, she unleashed upon us the wrath of Claudette – one of the most devastating weather cyclones to make landfall in Mauritius in fifteen years. Claudette's destructive force pummelled our breezy vacation let throughout the night, scaring the living hell out of both of us. But despite her best efforts to disrupt our relationship, the experience served to strengthen our bond.

In Cape Town, South Africa, a little more than a year later, we were married.

After the wedding, we moved to a beautiful little town on the south coast of Natal where I got absorbed into the testosterone-fuelled culture of a large bridge construction team. Jenni, on the other hand, bought and operated a health and fitness studio exclusively for ladies. At home, we struggled to reconcile our different outlooks. Jenni's love of form clashed with my obsession with function. The temporary nature of construction projects led me to view spends on curtains, carpets and the like as wasteful. Instead, I believed in spending only on essentials...like a belter of a hi-fi stereo system. At least when time allowed us, we could party like there was no tomorrow.

As time wore on, though, I became increasingly unsettled about living in a permanent state of transition and wanted something different. When I had chosen to study engineering, I had known deep down that it would be an imperfect fit. In wanting to 'do the right thing', I had suppressed my inner voice and allowed myself to be guided by peer pressure and the advice of others. Now my inner voice began to speak up. I reflected that whereas my working life had always revolved around things, my heart desired to experience working with something infinitely more challenging and exciting – people.

The defining moment came in the midst of a torrential downpour, late at night out on site. I decided it was time for a change. I left my job in construction and headed back to the University of Cape

Town to embark on a year of intensive full-time study towards an MBA degree.

Jenni found an hourly-paid job as an aerobics instructress, running up to five high-intensity classes a day just to take care of our living expenses. It was exhausting work for her but, my goodness, she was fit!

The year flashed past, and after graduating, I joined a huge multinational in the sales and marketing division. Loving the change, I eagerly looked forward to realising my passion for working with, motivating and directing people. Life was good and, not wanting to mess with that, I easily suppressed any ideas of starting a family. That is, until the tenth anniversary of our marriage.

On that red letter day, Jenni pronounced, with uncharacteristic forcefulness approaching that of Cyclone Claudette, that the time to start a family had finally arrived and further delay was not an option. I had no choice but to do the honourable thing.

Our beautiful baby Bianca was born in Cambridge during a short work assignment to the UK. Some four years later, back in Cape Town, our wonderful son Casey arrived to complete our much desired 'pigeon pair'.

However, I had precious little time for playing happy families over the next ten years with my focus on climbing the corporate ladder. To enhance my CV, I took on various roles in distribution, project management and technology. My work ethic was noticed and I landed an expatriate assignment to the corporate headquarters in London. Our family association with England, where I was also born and raised as a child, was about to be renewed. We lived very comfortably and wanted for absolutely nothing, except that increasingly elusive commodity – family time together.

My new programme management role had me shuttling – at one stage weekly – between London and the United States, where the company was piloting the development of a web-based software solution for international roll-out. It was a challenging and exhausting time for me. For Jenni, it meant devoting herself to the kids and, on weekends, picking up the pieces of a frequently shattered husband.

The aftermath of the dot-com collapse caused the members of our Project Steering Board to grow increasingly cautious. After eighteen months – and despite solid progress with the pilot project – they pulled the rug on the programme, and with it, my job.

Fortunately, as that door closed, another opened. I was assigned a senior management role in IT. Although hugely thankful for the lifeline, I was inwardly disconcerted. My career path had U-turned away from my passion – working with people. The steel and concrete of my past had been replaced by bits and bytes.

At about that time, my company flip-flopped in its policy towards leadership development. Functional specialists, previously disadvantaged in selection for leadership positions, would now be favoured over all-rounders. In other words, deep expertise in one field would be preferred to broad exposure in numerous fields.

It hit me like a ton of bricks. For twenty years I had sweated to gain the wide exposure seen as crucial for advancement only to find that the game had changed. I learnt a salutary lesson. It was finally time to start playing my own game, doing what I loved rather than what I thought was expected of me. That change of heart soon attracted an exciting new opportunity.

The IT division embraced a radical cost reduction programme that necessitated the appointment of an internal communications manager to help build trust and two-way engagement between leadership and the employees. In simple terms, this was a role that involved working with and inspiring people. I jumped at the chance to apply, relying on pure passion – and a little help from the universe – to land the job. Having the courage to follow my heart felt exciting, invigorating and liberating.

Over the next three years I became totally immersed in my great new job and was soon asked to join the corporate communications team and manage internal communications for the entire organisation. Despite exciting developments on the work front, though, my life transformation was still far from complete with the 'holy grail' of quality family time beyond my grasp. It was time for another curveball from the universe.

With my assignment drawing to a close, my thoughts turned to the future. With a major restructuring of the subsidiary, job prospects in South Africa looked bleak, so I enquired about the chances of permanent employment in the UK. To my great relief, I received a very positive response. Eager to share the good news with Jenni, I left work early, for once.

Jenni's reaction to my news, though, was as shocking as it was straightforward.

'Six years is long enough, Bill. It's time for the family to go home (to South Africa). My mind is made up. Now you must decide if you want to join us.'

I had clearly failed to 'read the tealeaves' while living in my work bubble. Realising that time had just been called on my career as I knew it, I felt anxiety, uncertainty and even resentment wash over me.

The universe knew differently.

Up until then, I had been financially supporting a close relative who had fallen on hard times. In her wisdom, seeing little improvement in the situation, Jenni suggested channelling our support into hiring a life coach.

Great idea, I thought, *but what on earth is a life coach?* Embarrassed with myself, I turned to Google.

To cut a long story short, my research culminated in a helpful meeting with Neil, the owner of a life coach training company and a man with whom I enjoyed instant rapport. As I looked to close the conversation by thanking him for his advice, he surprised me by turning his attention firmly to me.

'Bill, it's clear you're facing a great deal of change on a number of fronts in your life. I strongly recommend that you give life coaching a try for yourself.'

Neil insisted on connecting me with Sharon, a young Manchester-based life coach who had graduated from his training programme. With more than a little scepticism, I agreed to a series of telephone coaching sessions with her.

To my great surprise — and to Neil's and Sharon's eternal credit — I was blown away by the sheer power and simplicity of the coaching programme she skilfully guided me through. Shaking with excitement, I called Neil and got straight to the point.

'I absolutely love life coaching. It's simple, it works and it's life-changing. I'd love to introduce this training in South Africa — how about it?'

We concluded a deal and, in due course, Neil and his lovely wife Natasha flew to South Africa to help start up my new company, New Insights Africa. Neil and Natasha quickly identified in Jenni a natural coaching ability and passion, and Natasha channelled a lot of effort into coaching Jenni in the application of their life coaching system. In the space of just a few months, Jenni and I went from being ships in the night – sacrificing quality time together for the trappings of my corporate career – to being jointly involved in our own successful life coach training business.

Today I'm privileged to own New Insights, both in South Africa and the UK. Whereas I run the business and training side, Jenni provides coaching services to trainee coaches. As you may expect, we bring different yet complementary skills and perspectives to the business table.

A few years ago, I felt the time was right to do something I had long dreamed of doing. I wrote and published a book. It wasn't about building bridges (of the concrete sort), succeeding in corporate life or even starting a small business. I wrote about awakening to the magic of the life you love – a personal development book based on my journey to find and live my life purpose.

The cover page of the quirkily titled *A Boerewors Roll for the Soul* (boerewors is a type of traditional South African sausage) features a little creature that Jenni long ago adopted as a symbol of her own spirituality: the humble yet exquisite butterfly. It now symbolises my deep thanks and appreciation to Jenni for the role she played in my transformation and our coming together.

Jenni's Perspective – From Human Doings To Human Beings

When you know better, you do better.
Maya Angelou, Mentor to Oprah Winfrey

I don't think there are many people who haven't at some point in their life said, 'I wish I had known then what I know now.'

I've said this many times, but I know now that this wish is not my wish. If I had known, I would never have embarked on my amazing journey of self-realisation and evolving consciousness.

I believe that managing the energy of thought, perception and the linked emotions is the key to a fulfilled and happy life. When you truly understand that your 'doing' is a direct result of your thoughts and emotions, only then can you take full responsibility for your life experiences.

And then it comes to 'being'. I finally learnt that love, joy, peace and happiness are states of being that you can **choose**. The choice comes with a consciousness while **in** the present moment, the awareness **of** the moment, and the thoughts you hold **about** the moment.

It all makes perfect sense, and the processes are simple and empowering. Yet many people get so busy with life and ego-jostling and wanting to be right that they forget who they are at the deepest level.

This wasn't clear to Bill and me in those early days. We used to argue and fight about reality. I 'had my head in the clouds' and 'needed to get down to earth, and he 'just didn't get it'. Of course, I was going to expect miracles – who wouldn't? And here, the fire and water signs made steam.

Bill and I and our children have had many memorable experiences together – some fabulous and some not so much. However, each experience contained within it a lesson and an opportunity to learn and grow, but only as long as we were prepared to do the work.

One particularly significant experience was our time spent in England. We embarked on an adventure that was to last six years – three years longer than originally planned. It was exciting, with so many things to discover: a new country, a new home and wonderful travel opportunities which took us to France, Spain, Greece, Antigua, Tobago and the Maldives. We lived more than comfortably. The kids were enrolled at a wonderful school; we had everything we wanted, and almost everything we needed.

What was missing was a wholesome family life. Bill's corporate career outpaced my life with the children and, as he has said, we were 'ships passing in the night' with very little time together. There were days when I felt filled with gratitude for the beautiful English countryside; for our magnificent manor house and exquisite garden with roses, daffodils, ponds and ducks. And then there were days when the loneliness caught up with me, and I ached for the familiarity and rhythm of Africa.

I was stuck, facing a conundrum. In England, I had everything I needed in the world of form. Yet spiritually, I felt incomplete, and my need for love and connection was not being met. I tried really hard to keep afloat and grateful, putting my everything into the children so that they felt whole while their father was absent. But I knew that this life of imbalance was not sustainable. It was especially obvious at bedtime when Bianca and Casey longed for Bill to read them stories and kiss them goodnight. I yearned to run barefoot on African soil again. I got to a point where I was more than happy to give up all the stuff in order to live according to my highest values of balance and family.

And so, after much ado, we returned to Cape Town. Bill has described the sequence of events leading up to his massive leap from corporate life to running life coach training companies in South Africa and the UK. And here we are! Bill runs the business using his people, communication and marketing skills brilliantly, and I am now a life coach. I call my practice 'True Essence Coaching'. It's my mission to help my clients find **their** true essence, as I have, in order to live authentically and consciously. My inner and outer purposes are finally aligned.

Bill and I will never be the same, and we don't want to be the same, but we are now getting into step on the Path of Life.

WOW

Joy is the result of a coming together
of heart and mind.

Uncertainty comes before progress
take a leap of faith

PaulLowe**HEARTS**

A Successful Life Of Service

JOHN BATTERBY

(Spain)

In offering an overview of my life so far, giving insights into my journey, I believe the best place to start is to define what prosperity means to me: achieving whatever goals I set out to achieve and being the very best I can be. On that basis, it's fair to say I live a life of prosperity in Spain and have done so for the past twelve years, although there have been one or two significant challenges along the way, including going to war at sixteen and being involved in two divorces, as well as a massive identity crisis at the age of forty-one.

I was born on 13 April 1965 and bred in Sheffield – an industrial working-class part of England. Although my family wasn't rich by any stretch of the imagination, my two younger sisters, Claire and Louise, and I were a happy bunch and always felt well provided for, loved and protected.

My mother was a strict disciplinarian and worked as a secretary at a local carpet shop. Dad, whom we seldom saw as kids, was a hard working self-employed painter and decorator and a typical northerner.

He would normally pop into the local pub for a pint after work, and the only time we really saw him was when he'd come home to say night-night before bedtime and during the two or three family holidays abroad that we were lucky enough to have most years.

A strong work ethic and honesty were values that were instilled in us as youngsters, and these are things that I still hold close to my heart today. I suppose that's why I've never understood people with talent not having that work ethic. Talent is nothing without taking the necessary action to make things happen.

At school, I was academically lazy – I left with two O-levels in Physics and Cooking. I was interested in becoming a chef, but wasn't sure how to achieve it. My grandfather was in the Coldstream Guards, but he died when my mother was nine. I think it was because of him that I always had the idea of being in the military to fulfil a career that he wasn't able to.

My mother was worried about what I was going to do, so she made enquiries and took the initiative to organise my first interview with the Royal Navy. This took place in December 1979 with me not yet fifteen years of age. Upon leaving school on Friday 29 May 1981, I travelled from Sheffield Railway Station, and fewer than forty-eight hours later arrived in Plymouth (in the south-west of England) to begin what would become a long and distinguished Naval career on Monday 1 June.

My first introduction to Navy life was the barber politely – and, upon reflection, sarcastically – asking me which parts of my long, curly hair I'd like to keep. After I had meticulously explained which bits were OK to cut and which bits needed styling, he duly shaved the lot off down to the bone. I entered the Navy as a trainee chef and did six weeks' basic training and a further six to seven months' trade training, then I was posted to HMS *Cochrane* in Scotland.

After five years as a chef, I re-categorised to become a Royal Navy Clearance Diver. Part of this trade involved EOD (Explosive Ordnance Disposal/Bomb Disposal), but this came after the 'small' task of being involved in warfare.

The Falklands War (2 April – 14 June 1982) was a military conflict between Great Britain and Argentina on the issue of sovereignty over the Falkland Islands. The British eventually surrounded the Argentine troops at the capital, Port Stanley, and forced them to surrender. At the time, the general understanding was that we were only going there as a warning to the Argentinians. We in the Navy were led to believe that by the time we got there, it would have all blown over. Furthermore, because of my tender years I shouldn't have even been on the ship, going into a potential conflict. However, I sailed on HMS *Brilliant* from 2 April 1982 to 14 June 1982 and hadn't even finished my training before I was involved in the harsh realities of war.

I was the youngest member to serve in the Falklands – at sixteen turning seventeen – and this taught me some monumental life lessons. At the time, in my immaturity and ignorance I thought of it all as a game, which I now realise protected me massively from experiencing the fear and trauma that many of my colleagues suffered. At that age I thought I was invincible, although I now concede my flippant attitude towards the possibility of dying was more down to naivety than any great courageous awareness, the reality being that I was far too young to understand the dangers. I'd comfort grown men in their late twenties and early thirties after constantly observing them break down and cry, but it was difficult for me to understand. I suppose the modern-day term would be 'ignorance is bliss'.

With heart-wrenching casualties on both sides – the inevitable conse-quence of war – we lost a few guys on our ship and others got injured with shrapnel and burns. After the trials and tribulations of the conflict, we arrived back in the UK and were given a heroes' welcome, which we didn't expect. There were thousands of people everywhere, fireworks going off and a real party atmosphere. We were all allowed a phone call – I phoned my dad because it was his birthday and announced, 'Happy Birthday, Dad, we've won. I'm on my way home.'

He simply replied, 'Good lad.'

It was on the back of the Falklands War that I decided I wanted to be more than just a chef. I wanted to achieve more with my life. As someone who believes in the power of having a positive mindset, I would say this experience was a magnificent challenge. In later years, the reflection of the events in the Falklands acted as a strong way of re-enforcing my 'have no regrets and live for today' attitude. Despite all the pain and suffering that war inevitably offers, I was grateful to have served.

In terms of my awareness towards pain, my life has always been black and white – obviously significantly conditioned by my years of extensive service and training within the Royal Navy, ranging from being a chef to the demands of Clearance Diving (there were still three quarters of a million mines from World War 2 around the British shores that needed diffusing) and being part of a Field Gun Crew. The Royal Navy's Field Gun Competition is a contest between teams from various Royal Navy commands in which sailors compete to transport a field gun and its equipment over and through a series of obstacles in the shortest possible time. This was the highlight of my Royal Naval career, the ultimate test. Although it involved extremely hard physical training for weeks on end, it was the epitome of efficient team-working and contributed massively towards my identity as someone who could always be relied upon and would never let anyone down.

After twenty-five years, my time was served. I was pensioned off from the Royal Navy at the ripe old age of forty-one. Now I suppose many people may think that to have been able to serve my country with distinction and then have a nice pay off at the end would be a great situation. It wasn't. I became confused about what to do each day. All certainty had been removed. I'd been part of a regimented institution where I was so well looked after – fed, clothed and everything was done for me. Repetition and routine and following disciplined orders had been my life for a quarter of a century. Now I was like a rabbit caught in the headlights, not knowing what to do next. Worse still, I felt as if I didn't know who I was or where I was going. Not only had I lost my identity, but my purpose in life, too. The whole transformation process was very difficult, and I instinctively knew that if I was to have any chance of recapturing my previous positive outlook, I needed a clean break and new goals.

To compound things, I was going through a messy divorce. Consequently, I decided to emigrate to Spain to get away from it all and restart my life. Interesting how fate steps in and offers alternative paths when we need them most.

Newly-landed in Spain, I faced one of the lowest times I'd had for a long time. I was mindful that I needed to get a job and was thinking, *What am I going to do?* After doing a few menial things, I bumped into a guy at the local pool who was an ex-Irish Ranger, so in a roundabout way the military helped me out. He was setting up a security company, we got talking and became business partners.

I built upon this successful business. I've always had a keen interest in health and fitness, so in 2010 I took a course and became a fully-qualified Personal Trainer.

It's amazing how you can condense a whole lifetime's diverse experiences under a few simple headings. Having recently become aware of the Three Pillars of Life Learning – Loving – Legacy approach, I can easily make sense of these key areas within my own brilliant service-driven voyage.

Learning. We learn something every day, no matter how minimal it is, even if it's on the back of something bad. Life's journey is a learning curve. Having goals and new achievements to work towards and constantly wanting to improve myself has provided me with huge benefits.

Loving. My self-love and self-belief are by-products of my secure family upbringing. Because of my extensive military training – particularly in bomb disposal – I had almost become a robot. I've been trained to detach myself from being too emotional – I switch myself off, and even now I'm aware that I'm still not back to being who I truly am.

Legacy. This is all about being remembered for something. For me, it's being positive. My glass is always half-full, never half-empty, and I have no regrets. I simply want to be remembered for being 'smiling John' – sharing my attitude with people and generally helping them the best way I can. That legacy means more to me than leaving millions of pounds, buildings or institutions behind.

I am now secure in my identity of being someone who will always be of good service to others. I'm certainly not a 'people-pleaser', but I am a bit of a soft touch and do like to help people out and see them happy. My vision is quite simple: to live a long, healthy, happy life and achieve many goals. I only wish my beloved football team – Sheffield United – could manage to excel in the field of achieving goals!

Life could have been so much more difficult. I've witnessed colleagues struggle post-war and post-service career, with many ending up homeless. I know my values of health, happiness, positivity, loyalty and truthfulness have been a constant source of strength and guidance for me.

WOW

Always strive to be positive no matter how big the challenge, because it will serve you multi-fold along your journey through life.

If you spent all your time looking in the car's rear-view mirror – as you travel on your journey – you'd crash.

So why do you expect different results as you travel on your own life's journey and keep dwelling on the past?

PaulLowe**HEARTS**

Family, Forest And Froth

JOHN 'SMUDGER' SMITH
(UK)

I was born and bred in inner-city Nottingham, England in the late 1940s as part of a large family. I started school in the early fifties and spent the rest of my life being judged and labelled by 'better' people than me, often wondering about the Good Samaritan and that old saying 'all that glitters is not gold'. So perhaps the opposite is true and all that doesn't glitter may be gold?

As someone who has been in the 'system' for the vast majority of my (almost) three-score and ten years, I am left to conclude there have been three powerful and consistent influences in my life – family, Nottingham Forest Football Club and booze – that have combined to provide me with pleasure and pain in equal amounts.

On my first day at school, my teacher took me into the cloakroom and said, 'Now then, this is your coat peg where you will keep your coat and PE bag.'

I still remember my startled horror and disgust as I retorted, 'I don't want a coat peg, cos I ain't ****ing stopping!' While I cringe now at my crude response, this was normal for me at the time. My upbringing was based upon nothing more than raw, brutal survival.

At play time that morning, I escaped to visit a nearby pond where two graceful swans were residing. Over a period of time, the swans got to know and trust me, and I used to feed them on bread that I'd pinched from the Tuck Shop. This pond became a haven for me. I'd paddle in it and pretend I was an Indian and I would kill all the cowboys I could (I wanted to be an Indian because all the other kids always wanted to be cowboys). Then in the afternoon, I'd make my way home and pretend I'd been to school all day, escaping the wrath of my dad who would invariably be upstairs, sleeping off the booze.

I remember him once saying he was like Robin Hood – he stole from the rich and gave to the poor. Even in my infancy, I wasn't convinced that his motives were entirely selfless. Once, he broke into a stocking factory and nicked thousands and thousands of pairs of them, resulting in practically every woman in Nottingham having enough of the damn things to last her months.

My mam said my older brothers were out of control so she had them sent away to children's homes. I lived with my grandmother and I once asked where Mam went all day and all night.

She simply replied, 'You'll understand when you're older.'

Because Dad was always in and out of prison, we didn't have much money so I started stealing. At first, it was just small things from shops, then I hit on a brainwave. About three streets away from our house was a coal yard, so I decided I could follow my dad's Robin Hood example and supply the entire neighbourhood at a cheaper rate.

At first it was OK, then it seemed like hard work – I needed an easier enterprise. My conditioning for stealing was ever-growing; I know

now I was creating a certain belief system around my identity, and this was galvanised by a simple need to survive. I progressed on to bigger things like breaking into shops and offices.

By now, the money was starting to come in. I would wait for my gran to go to sleep, and then I would deposit some of my ill-gotten gains into her purse. I think she'd rumbled me, though, because she'd often assert, 'One day, you'll end up in Bagthorpe' (Nottingham Prison).

One morning, my mam said I could go to Juvenile Court with her to see one of my brothers. I was about nine years old at the time and was really excited at the prospect. When we got there, a policeman told me it would be alright for me to go downstairs to the cells and visit my brother.

I jumped at the chance, but my elation soon turned to despair as the copper said to me, 'I don't think you understand, son. You are being sent away as well because your Mam doesn't want you, and besides, you keep missing school.'

I felt frightened and betrayed like never before.

I got to the children's home about tea-time and I can still vividly recall – with delight – my first meal of egg, chips and peas, with jelly for afters. I thought, *This is posh, cos I've never had jelly before.*

I was moved from home to home and never found love or happiness anywhere. When I was about thirteen, some mates and I stole 24,000 cigarettes. We each carried 6,000 apiece in large cardboard boxes back to Nottingham on the bus. As we proceeded to get rid of the stash, someone grassed on us, so I decided to go on the run to Chesterfield (a nearby area). I headed for a pub that all the villains and prostitutes used to frequent; I was 'advised' I'd be safe there.

The woman who ran the pub was an old-ish lady and she used to take 'clients' upstairs. I recall with disgust how some of the men wanted me to watch the 'performances', and some even wanted me to join in. To me then, this was all perfectly normal, though, because my own mam had always carried on this way.

The men used to get me drunk, and I still remember sipping my first pint of beer through the huge frothy head at the top of the glass, thinking, *This stuff's good – I could get addicted to it.*

Eventually I returned to Nottingham, and Mam had left my dad. His drinking had become even worse. Because Mam was no longer there to see to his intimate comforts, he started to molest me. He said it would be alright so long as I never told anyone, but I instinctively knew this wasn't right, so I deliberately got caught on a job to be sent as far as possible away from my dad.

Over the years, the crime continued, with my early motive of providing money for Gran long-since gone. By now, I was consumed by anger, hatred and a total lack of self-esteem. I was carrying an immense amount of toxic venom towards my parents for teaching me this way of life and setting me on the road to despair and destruction. The realisation that my mam was a whore and my dad was a nonce (child molester) caused me immense suffering, let alone pain, and this self-hatred carried on well into my thirties.

Then a dramatic event changed my life.

I was in prison in the middle of another sentence for burglary when a close friend on the outside committed suicide. I totally immersed myself in victim mode – I just wanted to die, blaming myself for his death because it wouldn't have happened if I'd been there, right?

Wrong!

This misery and suffering continued, turning to depression. The guilt remained with me for some time until one Sunday – out of total desperation – I attended the prison chapel. For the first time in my perceived miserable existence, I began to feel shame about my crimes. I cried over and over again with genuine remorse and vowed I would make amends to society once I was free.

These formative decades of my life gave me an extremely negative perception of what family life was all about. The events that unfolded over the ensuing years could not have been more contrasting. Family became the glue that gave my life meaning and purpose – still with challenges, though.

I first met my ex-wife Alice – who already had three children – in 1979, and the relationship progressed to the point that we had our own beautiful daughter, Collette, in 1980. Three years after this elation-filled event, Alice was raped, and my responsibility, as I saw it, was to protect my family and seek revenge. I managed to find out where the cowardly scum lived and set about my task. Upon arriving at his place, I kicked the door in and stabbed him in his balls – I wanted to make sure he wouldn't rape anyone else. For this, I got a five-and-a-half year prison sentence, while the rapist got three years – for three rapes. Justice eh?

As soon as I came out in 1987, I got custody of Collette because Alice and I had split up while I was in prison. My daughter and I were blissfully happy, although we didn't have many possessions and I had hardly any money to support us, initially.

I managed to get painting and decorating jobs and was absolutely determined that Collette would enjoy a warm, loving and secure childhood – something I'd never had. This continued for years, and my daughter has turned out to be a beautiful, well-balanced soul with two kids whom I worship and adore.

Later in life, I met a lady called Carol, and the universe conspired to repeat itself and grant us a beautiful baby girl – Shannon. My two amazing daughters, as well as my step-children with Alice, have been a powerful force of love, and I know without doubt that they have given me a reason to live and a purpose.

As a kid, I was constantly labelled as illiterate, and was advised on one of my juvenile detention centre 'holidays' to find something that interested me. Consequently, I started researching all professional football clubs in England so that I could better understand my passion around the one that I loved – Nottingham Forest FC. While I was in prison, Nottingham Forest was my reason for living – along with my beautiful daughter, Collette – and I now rationalise this as me creating a sense of identity; needing to be part of a tribe and belong.

In 1959, Forest reached the FA Cup Final at Wembley – every football supporter's dream – and my dad promised to take me. However, the bastard – as usual – let me down and went with all his boozing mates instead. All was not lost, though; the guy at the local fish and chip shop gave me a load of batter bits to compensate!

Years later, fate ensured I met up with Psycho – not the Forest legend Stuart Pearce, but the author of this book, Paul Lowe. I gave him that name because of his fearless attitude and his never-say-die spirit. He is unlike anyone I've ever known, including all my borstal and prison acquaintances.

Forest wasn't the only thing we had in common – we both had serious drink addictions and we'd spend hours talking about our tortured pasts and how one day we might enjoy a different life. I started drinking at thirteen to numb the pain and suffering of my shameful existence.

As I enter the twilight of my challenging life, my one big regret is that I missed so many years of my kids' and step-kids' upbringing.

The legacy I leave, though, is I managed to break the parent abuse and neglect cycle, and as a result, all my years of learning and paying my debts to society have meant my kids haven't had to. I'm so proud of them all and love them immeasurably.

WOW

Never underestimate the power of love.

The F-Factor

LUCIE BRADBURY
(UK)

When exploring the recipe for feminine entrepreneurial success (the F-Factor), I often find the missing ingredient is consideration of the external conditions that underpin success (or lack of it), and the link between those and women's ability to sustain the kind of success that they want.

Most people don't focus on their external conditions. But if a fish is sick, what would you do – change the fish or the water? The logical answer is change the water. Why? Because the fish is only as healthy as the water it swims in.

I want to help women stop trying to change themselves and start changing the water.

Think of these four questions: why are your external conditions important? What are the right external conditions for you to find your F-Factor? How do you create those conditions? What happens if you can't create the right conditions?

It was like being at my own funeral as I stared out of the window, watching all my friends enjoying my thirtieth birthday party. I was living a life that I knew I didn't want any more. I was immensely grateful to have been given a second chance, but every moment I spent wasting it broke my heart. Something drastic needed to change, but I didn't know what or how.

I didn't want to run away – I'd just come back from a year-long around the world trip, so the answer didn't lie 'out there'. But how could I stay in a place that I didn't seem to belong in any more? A place where people didn't get me, were tired of my story and gave me that 'there she goes again' look. My well-meaning friends wanted me to get back to normal – working hard all week and partying all weekend. I had a great career and the trappings of success, but something told me there had to be more to life than this.

That was back in 2002. Six months earlier I'd had a huge wake-up call in a car accident while travelling in Australia. Two friends lost their lives – I was one of the lucky ones.

While I lay still and waited for the paramedics to cut me free (I'd broken my neck), I asked myself a question: 'If I die right now, if this is to be the end of my life, have I done what I came here to do?'

In that moment, I knew I hadn't. I knew that despite my success, I was wasting my life. I made a promise – if I was given another chance to live, I would commit to thriving and fulfilling my true potential.

That accident taught me three things that changed my life:

- I was here for an important, unique and special reason
- All the answers are within me (I just needed to ask better questions)

- We are all connected and I would never really be alone again

I knew that for me to thrive, I needed to live my life on **purpose**, step into my **power** and only then would I fulfil my **potential** and allow myself to **profit** from it (in every sense). My intention for this chapter is to help you to do the same and show you a system to keep doing it.

Despite my promise after my initial wake-up call, I recovered from my injuries and life just went back to normal. And being surrounded by 'normal', I found it hard to make progress. I wished for things to be different, but I didn't seem to be able to make it happen. I knew I deserved more, but it felt like I was walking through treacle, getting nowhere fast. Back then, change was hard. To make matters worse, on paper I appeared to have everything, and nobody could understand my problem, least of all me. So, I did what I'd always done and nothing changed.

I kept searching, though – I hadn't been through that accident and broken my neck for nothing – and then my breakthrough came.

It came in the form of a personal development seminar, and more crucially, a group of people who finally got me. I discovered that there were other people who felt just like I did. It was like coming home.

These people didn't question me – they asked me great questions. They didn't judge me – they opened my eyes to new possibilities. They didn't want me to pretend to be anyone else, and they helped me become more of the real me.

The reason we often do not reach our potential is because we're not doing what we know we need to do. So why is that? For me, it was my lack of self-belief and support – and those two things were linked.

When I surrounded myself with mentors and entrepreneurs who believed in me, I burst through my limitations and thrived. Being in this environment helped me to accelerate what was inside me. I learned the importance of creating the right conditions for me to grow.

If we're stuck, we often need an external stimulus to shake us out of our trance. We need references, examples of what's possible, to help us to see the world through new eyes that will give us the courage to change. This is the value in having a support system, mentors and a peer group that will encourage us to a higher standard and hold us there. I discovered that another P – **peer group** – makes the difference between truly thriving and merely surviving.

Imagine you are surrounded by people who really get you, support you and encourage your aspirations even when you are scared. They believe in you before you believe in yourself. How might that affect your success? Or even how much you enjoy your success? How might that support and accelerate your growth? You arrive in this world with an amazing, unique and special talent. At first, being you is enough and everything you do is amazing. Imagine if you carried on growing in an environment where everything you did was amazing – do you think you would have more confidence or less? Would you do more with your life, make faster, quicker decisions if you weren't going to hear 'I told you so' if things didn't work out?

Changing your conditions changes everything.

Despite my good intentions, it was only when I changed my conditions, and especially my peer group, that my life really changed. Then I felt compelled to find a solution for my clients, and I created 'Damsels in Success' so that women would have access to a unique level of support and development on a continuous basis and a real chance of sustainable success. As entrepreneurs, we are not on an average path, and our environments and lifestyles need to reflect that. I refer to this as our **place** in life and it's about where we hang out. It includes what's around us and what's inside us. What we feed our environment (and that includes our mind and body) gives us the fuel to accelerate our progress.

I meet and work with a lot of women in the Damsels in Success community, and when I meet a woman who is thriving, I just know. It's not a scientific measure, but if someone is feeling and looking alive, they will have a sparkle in their eyes that speaks to my heart.

Women who are thriving might tell me things like 'I am so excited, I'm doing what I love' and that they feel 'extremely valued' for doing it. They demonstrate that they live in line with their values and are authentically content with their lot. Despite their success, I usually find these people are the most open – they never say, 'I've heard that before' or that they are beyond or above anything. They are willing to learn and share their own secrets. This is infectious, and any woman who wants success wants to be around other women who are doing the same. It's good to be around people who are further up the line than you in some areas, and others who will gratefully receive the wisdom you have to offer.

If 'life is our mirror' and our vibration is affected by everything around us, we need to consider the effect our space could be having. In order to have a thriving culture in which we can operate, we want to create an environment that lifts us, fills us up and gives us energy (rather than drains it).

In summary, when we have the following cultural conditions in place, we significantly increase our ability to THRIVE.

T	= Teacher
H	= Help and support
R	= Resources
I	= Inspiration
V	= Values
E	= Environment

One of my business mentors says, 'Ordinary things consistently done produce extraordinary results' (Cunningham, 2017).

I speak to many people who talk about their grand vision to change the world. It is the actions they take every day that will ground this into reality. A thriving culture is one that supports people in doing ordinary things consistently until they produce extraordinary results. Our environmental conditions fundamentally influence our ability to live out our **potential**, harness our true **power** so we and others can **profit** from it. By establishing things on **purpose**, having an empowering **peer group** and an enlightening **place,** we enable all of that to happen consistently and with ease.

These are the **Six Ps of Feminine Success.**

Before you create a plan to live fully and meaningfully, you first need to know where you currently are. Take a few minutes now to answer the following questions. Be as honest as you can about your current situation.

On a scale of 0–10 (10 being extremely well, 0 being not at all), how well do you:

Purpose:

- Live your life intentionally (with conscious awareness)?
- Do what you love?
- Love what you do?
- Live in alignment with your values?
- Have people around you who share those values?
- Have awareness when you are acting out of alignment and adjust quickly?

Power:

- Believe you can create anything that you want?
- Believe in the power of the group?
- Spend time with people who have done what you want to do (in the way that you want to do it)?

Potential:

- Have people around you who encourage your potential?
- Have people around you who expand or limit your thinking or behaviours and actions?
- Believe anything is possible?
- Invest in mentors/coaches who focus on your greatness?

Profit:

- Focus on adding value, and trust that the money will follow?
- Measure your success internally or externally?

- Surround yourself with people who have the kind of income that you have/would like to have?

Peer group:

- Consciously consider whom you spend the most time with?
- Feel able to ask for help?
- Have people around you who will encourage you, nurture your thoughts/ideas, hold you accountable, and give you tough love when you need it?

Place:

- Have a home/work space that reflects what's important to you?
- Consciously choose where you spend time, and change it if you feel stuck?
- Feed your mind with nurturing thoughts?
- Feed your body with nourishing food?
- Sleep well?
- Exercise/move your body frequently?

Thinking points summary:

- Think about these questions and consider the impact this chapter may have on you
- Is it possible you can live your life in alignment and love what you do?
- What is holding you back from creating everything you want?
- How can you invest in yourself to ensure you fulfil your potential?

- What will it look like when you have achieved success?
- Do you have a positive community in place to support you, nudge you and hold the space for you to turn your dreams into reality?

WOW

Surround yourself with a peer group that
supports your personal growth.

Embrace your feminine freedom;
it radiates light & warmth throughout the universe

PaulLoweHEARTS

Finding My Life's Purpose

JEPHIAS MUNDONDO

(Zimbabwe)

It is amazing that all human beings come into this world without any knowledge of what they have to do and why they are here. The individual human purpose remains hidden and only a few manage to find it.

In manufacturing, even the smallest gadget has an instruction manual, but unfortunately in the case of life – important as it is – there is no such manual to follow. This becomes a challenge to many people and they end up with life directing what they do rather than directing their own lives, never discovering their purpose and making it happen. The worst thing to do is to live other people's lives through copying and imitating or because we are trying to meet others' expectations. The real us will be there somewhere within, wondering what is going on.

This is a story of my journey from day one to where I am now, as I write. I call it my interesting journey. In this narration, I will be looking at how I found myself and my life purpose. There were no signposts – I could have followed them if they had been available. You could say how I got to where I am now was just by coincidence. However, I did manage to find my passion and purpose.

We grow up looking at people around us – siblings, friends, parents, teachers. From their experiences, we are influenced and sometimes advised, and from that advice we become what we end up being. When I look back, I could have unknowingly influenced my brothers, sisters and other children in the village, and subsequently my own children as well. But the process of admiring someone and following in their footsteps hinders many from finding their own life purpose.

The questions I asked myself were, 'Who really knows where I am meant to be going? What is my calling and purpose in life?'

Born into the third world, I arrived in Masvingo, a small town in Zimbabwe. It was so exciting going to school, and I reached a level where I could take a course so that I could find employment. Being educated was the number one value within our family and community and I couldn't have dodged that.

My father wanted me to be a handyman, specialising in household electrical work. I never liked it, but at the time I had no other option. After training, I got a job, but was not happy in it. I did not know my life purpose yet, so could not say to myself, 'Why am I doing this instead of something else?' I did not know what that something else was. The only good thing was that I was earning some money.

I changed my job and went into law enforcement. That was even worse, except I enjoyed the training, parade drills, helicopter drills, firing guns and the different life experiences. It was fun rather than purposeful and was more of an adventure than a career. Subconsciously I was still looking for the real thing.

After three years I left law enforcement and decided to go into agricultural management. The training was great and I really enjoyed working with animals. I ended up managing cattle and wildlife ranging operations. It was a good and interesting experience, and I even got a few 'Cattleman of the Year' awards for the company which I was working for.

It was during that phase that someone whispered to me about my life purpose. When my senior manager, Christie, called me to his office, I thought it was for the usual feedback on operations and the planning of our activities.

He sat me down in a way which he had never done before, saying he was going to tell me something which could be a bit disheartening.

'Jephias, you are not an agriculturist. You are doing the wrong job. You are supposed to be working with people.'

I looked at his face and saw an honest man saying something that he had been sent by the universe to say. But I was a bit stunned as that year I had won the 'Provincial Cattleman of the Year' award. How could such an achiever and a champion be in the wrong job?

I walked out of Christie's office and went back to mine. I couldn't concentrate on my work and decided to go home for an early lunch. I locked myself in my bedroom and asked myself various questions. What did Christie really mean? Didn't he like me? Did he want to push me out of this great organisation where I had done so well? Was he OK in the head? Was he drunk?

When our purpose is revealed to us, it often does not initially make any sense. We hold on to what we are doing at the time because it feels familiar and in our comfort zone. This is especially so when we do not know what our life purpose is meant to be. The question of whether there was anything better than what I was doing had never come into play in my mind. This could have been due to self-doubt and not knowing how far I could grow.

I spent the whole week thinking over the issue and could not come up with an answer. Then I asked to have a meeting with Christie, during which I asked him why he thought I wasn't an agriculturist and how I could move on to this new vision of his.

He said, 'Since you have managed the Estate, you have not had a labour dispute. You respect people, even those below you, love them and appreciate their service. You are a down to earth type of person.'

Down to earth? What is that?

I spent the whole week saying to myself, 'Jeph, down to what? To earth!' I reflected on my life to see what this down to earth was all about, comprehending that I was able to interact with all types of people at any level. I could listen to what people liked to chat about and understand if it was important to them. I always wanted to see myself as being just as human as anybody else despite being in a senior managerial position at work, but I never thought of it as my life's purpose. But if this was my down to earth, then Christie was right.

As Christie advised, I did my studies with the then Institute of Personnel Management, and passed really well. I was also interested in Labour Relations and Training, which I passed with distinctions. These newly-acquired qualifications enabled me to be employed in senior positions as I was now more marketable and I was officially given Human Resource management roles. On two occasions, I was headhunted for more senior positions and started to see what Christie meant.

I continued to pursue my studying ambitions and went ahead to do a Master's Degree in Development Management. That was when I realised that what was being taught in the programme resonated with my soul – helping the poor; negotiating for win-win situations; looking at things from the other person's point of view; making sustainable environmental decisions. I started recognising the 'down to earth' person whom I had been told about, and my studies strengthened the point.

Many questions came into my mind. Why had I never heard about this Development Management course before? Who was hiding it from me? Were my previous colleges not smart enough to know about that wonderful course? Were all the people I had met unaware? How great things are hidden from people in life is a real mystery, and how they discover what's hidden, if they do, is another mystery.

After finding myself, I was engaged as a Chief Executive Officer (CEO) of an organisation working on HIV/AIDS interventions in different communities. At that time, HIV was having a devastating effect in Eastern and Southern Africa. People were dying left, right and centre throughout all the communities. There was no treatment, no knowledge about prevention and no social support networks for children whose parents were dying of the virus. I had never seen children being orphaned at such a rate. It was worse than any war experienced in the region.

With all my heart, I served, working long hours; going through the pain of death – of losing parents, sisters, brothers and friends, and knowing more were going to perish with no treatment. It was like millions of people falling into a bottomless pit. At times I would close my office door and just sit there in tears as I asked, 'God, what should I do to make the biggest impact to save your people?'

Surprisingly, though, I was still energetic and had all the enthusiasm needed to serve and save my community.

As if HIV was not enough, the economic situation in the country was also melting down. This worsened the suffering for the infected and orphaned children. It was only later that treatment was accessed, mainly through funding partners from Europe, the United Kingdom and America.

After ten years, I felt I had completed my calling and took early retirement. This was the agriculturalist who was told to leave growing maize and breeding cattle and move on to working with people. The level of satisfaction I had when I retired was so great, I really felt I had achieved what very few people would have been able to do in ten years. I had answered my call to serve when I was needed. This was going to be an honour I would carry throughout the rest of my life and my heart was filled with joy.

I had found my purpose and fulfilled it.

From answering one calling, I felt the urge to answer another. While serving as the CEO of the Family AIDS Caring Trust, I had thought of becoming a Life Coach. Influenced by a Life Coach who trained us when I was a Board Member of the Regional AIDS Training Network, I decided to train.

Another surprise – what was this Life Coaching thing? I had heard of a Soccer Coach and had indeed been one, but a Life Coach was a new animal in my world. Where was this precious knowledge hiding? Here I was, learning things I should have learned when I was in school.

The training changed me and I gained far more in my own life than just becoming a certified Life Coach. My mind was stretched to levels I never thought existed in this world, learning about how to use resources, set goals, milestones and essential action steps towards achieving them, and about how to break down negative beliefs to embrace new, positive, empowering ones. I learned about uncovering the hidden rules we set for ourselves, projection and effective communication, responsibility and the true meaning of life. How not to be judgemental; how to be more creative and understanding; how the human mind works; how we create our realities through our thinking.

Changing my thinking changed my life. Having grown up in both Traditional African and Christianity religions, I'd always believed someone else was to blame if something went wrong – Satan, demons, the guy next door and even ancestors were responsible for any failures in life. If things didn't go well, I used to think it was because I was just unlucky. I had never previously known that my thoughts created my reality, or that I become what I think all day long.

I hadn't heard of the Law of Attraction – how I attract my own happiness, wealth, even good friends and good fortune. Measuring the advantages of positive thinking against the disadvantages of negative thinking, I built a castle in my mind, and being positive became one of my new characteristics which I've carried forward to this day. What a shift it was. The challenges were to live that life, teach that life and train more Life Coaches in my community.

I got into reading books which contained all the wisdom I had been deprived of – books like *Your Erroneous Zones*, *Virus of the Mind*, *The Power of Positive Thinking*, *Ask and It Is Given*, *Peace is the Way*, *Unlimited Power*, *Wishes Fulfilled*, *Inspired Destiny* and many others. I developed my mind and understood how to get what I want in life. My reading generated a hunger to write and I wrote articles in the local weekly paper for two and a half years.

My amazing journey from the farmer I used to be, to Life Coach and Life Coach trainer, was full of interesting experiences (despite not knowing where I was supposed to be going). It was more about following the wind. The shift from who I was to who I am, equipping myself to gain even more wisdom, still surprises me, and others. It makes me look back and ask myself how I got to be where and who I am now, examining my journey from less awareness to enlightenment.

After all my years of coaching people and seeing them become successful on the journey to finding their life purpose, moving from doubting to knowing, I'm now aware of my life purpose. It is to share wisdom, change lives, help people awaken to new thinking, empower people to realise their full potential and know that this life is full of possibilities.

WOW

You don't know what you don't know, so
forgive yourself your mistakes as you progress
along the exciting path of discovery.

Each moment presents an opportunity for growth grasp it and pass it on to others

PaulLowe**HEARTS**

Eyes Wide Open,
Heart Even Wider

LIZ BROWN
(UK)

Since I was a small girl, I have known that contributing to others is an important part of my essence. Being creative is a gift that I've denied and embraced at different times of my life, often finding it at the bottom of my priority list, even though it gave me such joy.

As a young girl, I had an adventurous, happy spirit. I loved being out on my bike with others. My career and life so far have provided me with wonderful times of achievement and pride. In the period when my two daughters were young, as a stay-at-home mum, I built a successful cake design business, creating hundreds of celebration cakes over two years. This self-taught business acumen built my confidence, self-esteem and developed my belief in my creative gift, as well as finding a niche market – delivering a product and service for that special day. Some twenty-five years later, customers I meet still recall and comment on Lizzie's Cake Kitchen and 'The Cake'.

In 2001 and 2003, I completed two long-distance cycle rides, which proved to be two of my best personal achievements, raising £12,000 for CLIC Sargent, a UK-based children's cancer charity. Everyone cycling had a personal reason for getting saddle sore, and I was no different – losing my brother-in-law and a dear friend in their twenties to cancer. The first cycle ride in 2001 was at a challenging time for me, and getting on my bike to train early in the morning, seeing and feeling the sunrise on my face, appreciating the space and warmth, my mind, body and spirit inspired, I was driven to succeed.

However, before I did my second cycle ride in 2003, I finally got divorced, was diagnosed with bladder cancer and made redundant, all within a twelve-month period. It felt like I had one wall after another to climb over. I had to dig deep and face both personal and financial challenges, but these were nowhere near what the families we were cycling for were facing.

Someone once told me that when you feel you are at your weakest, you are actually at your strongest. Vulnerability, mistakes, sadness, self-doubt and fear – I experienced all of these. However, in feeling these emotions and working through these trials, I discovered the opportunity to grow into me. I became conscious of my thoughts, feelings and a gritty determination which was simmering inside me, in time discovering an inner strength and belief to achieve more.

I was a single mum to two beautiful teenage daughters and working full-time, but I was determined to live life to the full and not look back down the path unless it was to power me forward. My wonderful family and friends stood just close enough to support me, but far enough back to give me the space to evolve and grow for myself — what a truly magnificent love to receive. It awoke a steely resolve deep within me and the energy to survive.

In 2007, I moved from a successful career in Financial Services. As I sat in a hospital bed recovering from another operation, I knew that if stress was adding to the condition, I needed to change my career path. At one time I had loved helping people move from A to B with their finances, but it had lost its shine. It no longer lit me up. However, I thought that if I'd helped people in that area of their life, I could help them get from A to B in other areas, so I trained as a Life Coach. For the next six years I worked with many leading lights in the UK Personal Development world.

In 2004, I met a wonderful man, Trevor, who became my husband in 2008. My family widened, my circle of friends grew, and he introduced me to his faith with the Salvation Army. I became involved with voluntary work there, cooking for the homeless. The spiritual connection between my coaching and my faith held me strong and gave me a true sense of contributing to all.

I haven't always understood the path my life took, but in recent years I have learned to trust and have faith that a Higher Power does. I also accept that it is my responsibility to take the steps needed to go forward.

In 2010, I was offered the opportunity to travel to the Amazon with the Pachamama Alliance, but I wasn't able to afford the cost. I was invited to go trance dancing – setting an intention and then dancing into it, engaging my energy and spirit. I set the intention 'If I'm meant to go to the Amazon, God will show me a way'.

That was on the Wednesday. On the Friday, I sold my previous house, which had been on the market for a year, and on the Monday I received a cheque for £8,000. My ticket was booked in minutes and I was off on the adventure, little realising the life-changing experience that awaited me.

Before I left, I stated the mantra, 'Eyes wide open, heart even wider'. I journeyed high into the Andes and deep into the Amazon. I received Shamanic healing sessions from elder Shamans, who read and cleared my energy channels from negative and trapped energy, which contribute to disease.

On my return to the UK, I was due to start a course of medical treatment. Confused, I asked the Shaman which one I should have – the Shamanic or the modern – and I was told to have the balance of both. The Achuars' (Amazonian community) vision of the Eagle (the technological age and the head) and the Condor (the ancient ways and the heart) flying together is the Sacred Dance. If people can embrace the two, the future will be full of golden opportunity for humanity.

I did exactly that – I had two Shamanic healing sessions and returned to have a series of modern infusions. I previously had not been able to go six months without surgery, but in October 2014, my bladder was classified as normal, and I've not had any further signs of cancer.

The Achuar is an intact dream culture. Achuar people had a vision that they should make an alliance with the very threat they feared – the outside world. They reached out, and that calling was heard and the Pachamama Alliance was formed (to bridge the native and modern worlds). The Achuar changed from a killing culture to a living culture, and created a partnership with their tribal neighbours and the modern world that could support them in protecting the rainforest and the way of life that they have lived for thousands of years.

*At first I thought I was fighting to save the rubber trees, and
then I thought I was fighting to save the Amazon rainforest,
now I realize I am fighting to save humanity.*

CHICO MENDES, ENVIRONMENTALIST

Visiting the Achuar Tribe deep in the heart of Mother Nature, I
experienced a true example of humanity where love, creativity and
family connection resonated, inspired and healed me. I discovered
and embraced the real me, getting reacquainted with my inner-child
and listening to my inner-voice challenging me to step up and claim
my vision to help make a difference to people's lives.

In 2015, Trevor was diagnosed with Hodgkin's Lymphoma. I
immediately wanted Trevor to have the same life-changing opportunity as I'd had in the Andes. I contacted a friend, a transference
healer who worked on Trevor's energy remotely. Another friend
recommended a Naturopath who read Trevor's energy fields, advised
us that the roots of the disease lay in pesticides and gave us an
organic and supportive eating plan. I gave him Reiki (a technique
for relaxation and reducing stress) every night before he fell asleep,
and we visited the Chalice Well in Glastonbury where he bathed
and drank the healing waters.

We believed we'd embraced the balance of the ancient and the NHS
(UK National Health Service) modern treatments. Trevor had a PET
scan, which showed him at stage three. He then started a six-month
course of chemotherapy. We both agreed we would not give any
power to the condition in our thoughts, believing that our thoughts
become our words, become our actions and then our reality.

On the bus going to Trevor's first appointment, we saw an advert
for a six-year BA (Bachelor of Arts) course in English Literature

and Community Engagement at Bristol University. There was to be an open day the next day. Trevor went along, and over the next few weeks he put in an application, was invited for an interview and then offered a place, which he accepted. This gave him a long-term goal to focus on, and an expectancy to survive the six years and be fit enough to complete the course.

At his next PET scan three months later, his results showed that the Sacred Dance had indeed played out. There was no sign of any cancer, but he had to complete the full six months' chemotherapy to be certain of eliminating any micro remainder.

We had always said that if anything happened to one of us, our house would be too large for the remaining one. Now we asked ourselves, 'Why are we waiting for one of us to die? Let's reduce our belongings, sell our house and make some memories together.'

Where are we today? We're living out our dream, vision, adventure – we bought a motorhome. We started exploring the UK on 1 September 2016 and are currently travelling for five months around Europe. We reduced our belongings by 60% and live a content, simple and happy lifestyle. We wake every morning grateful for each other; for the blessing of time, space and individual inner journeys while we're travelling together on our amazing adventure.

Trevor has just finished the second year of his six-year BA course, and we both work as we travel. Trevor focuses on property, and I create and host The Inner Artist retreats – space is created at unique luxury locations where guests retreat to be in nature, disconnecting from the digital world and the busyness of life for two days. There they can recharge, renew and reignite, building a bridge between their creativity and creator and reuniting with the natural them.

On our travels, we have had conversations with wonderful people, witnessed Mother Nature and learned many lessons from our experiences. We will continue to learn as we live in the present moment, knowing that tomorrow is not promised to anyone. As we travel, I'm writing about and photographing our trip. How this will evolve, I'm not sure, but creating a journal and art keeps our journey real, makes it exciting, and releases and expresses my flow in life. My desire for contribution led me to create 'The Inner Artist' on Facebook, a private group where people can engage with fellow creators – a wonderful community of artists, musicians, hat makers, chocolate makers, poets, authors, photographers, potters and many more all expressing their uniqueness in a non-judgmental space.

My mission is to make as many hearts sing and souls dance in the world as I can through love, creativity and transformation. My golden pathway is one where fellow travellers meet and journey while lighting the pathway for others to follow their creative hearts.

The Sacred Dance truly saved our lives and strengthened our core belief of love, faith, trust and peaceful living.

Join me at The Inner Artist
https://www.facebook.com/groups/132332243991070/
or follow me on Instagram or at http://liz-brown.net/

WOW

There is nothing more innovative than using creativity, time and space to transform people.

Open your eyes and hearts to all the
wonderment the world has to offer

PaulLoweHEARTS

Who Am I?

KEVIN SEARCEY
(UK)

I was born in the early 1960s in a rough but tightly-knit part of Nottingham, known as St Ann's. Although times were hard and the family was poor, this was only in a financial sense. I enjoyed a loving, secure childhood; one that contributed towards giving me the confidence to progress to a high level in karate and subsequently engage in many fight tournaments.

I suppose 'Who am I?' is one of those questions – along with 'What's the meaning of life?' – that many people ask themselves from time to time. I know this question has generally floated through my mind over the last twenty-five years or so.

Having been married for ten years, I found myself off work after severely damaging my right knee in a karate accident in 1993. As a result, money was scarce, and after many heated arguments, my wife (Janet) and I eventually spilt up in 1994. It was devastating for me to leave my two kids Paul and Kaylee behind. Soon after we split, I learnt that Janet was expecting our third child, Nicola being born in November 1994.

All I had in the world was a few clothes and a battered Robin Reliant estate car. The guy I had purchased it from used to race Reliants at stock car events and told me how fast it was. I found this to be true one day – coming back to Nottingham from Sheffield, I was stopped by the police for doing 90mph!

Now separated from my wife, I moved back in with my loving parents, who were extremely supportive and gave me food and shelter. I suppose this was the first time I became conscious of my identity question 'Who am I?' because I had gone from being a proud family man providing for his loved ones to someone who now needed his parents' support.

The ensuing months were painful in every imaginable way. Physically, I had to cope with knee operations and rehab, but this physical pain was absolutely nothing compared to the emotional suffering I was experiencing due to missing my children, whom I adored. Nothing seemed to go right. I was fighting for access to see my children, and I remember wondering daily when this fight was ever going to end. Missing my kids was made even harder by the fact I knew how much they missed me too. The arguments carried on and my kids seemed to be in the middle of it all.

Eventually, my ex-wife allowed my children to come and see me at my mum and dad's home. I have priceless memories of sitting there on a Saturday morning, watching *Saved By The Bell* and *Rugrats* with me in the middle of all my kids, eating their grandma's special toasties. In May, it was my birthday and I got some money from my family. All I could think of was using the cash to treat my kids to a McDonalds.

The year rolled by and the visits to the solicitors seemed never-ending. As 1994 was drawing to a close, I couldn't get the thought of having no money out of my head. I was determined to look after my kids for Christmas, so I reluctantly sold my beloved Reliant Robin.

January 1995 introduced itself and I recall wondering what this year would have in store for me. By now, I was feeling sorry for myself and completely in victim mode. I had a knee that kept giving way so had to wear a leg brace until the reconstruction later that year. My mind had become a myriad of negative ego-driven self-doubting thoughts; I really could not see a future, and anyway, what good would I be to my wonderful children? They deserved a better dad than I could ever be.

Other than it being my mum's birthday, 9 March 1995 was a significant date, because this was the day I thought I'd met my soulmate. I woke to the sun shining into my eyes through a gap in the blinds, dragged myself out of bed and duly wished my adoring mother a happy birthday. I was supposed to be going out that night with my friend Adrian, but I asked Mum if she'd phone him and relay that I couldn't make it because I was ill. Mum guessed what was really wrong with me: I was skint, but too proud to say so. She gave me a tenner and would not take it back, insisting that she just wanted to see me happy, going out and having a good time. Reluctantly, I rang Adrian to say I would go out later.

Later that evening we turned up at a place called Turner's – a little club above the local Mapperley Co-op store. We stood at the bar chatting away, but Adrian seemed to be preoccupied with looking at some ladies, commenting how pretty they were. To be honest, I remember not being interested. Or maybe I was just plain scared as I did not want to get hurt again. I felt like a fish out of water as I stood at the bar, sipping my pint and trying to look confident while Adrian talked to the ladies.

Then I glanced over at the dance floor and noticed a blonde woman who intrigued me. She seemed full of life and confidence as she walked towards her friends at the bar.

As Adrian and I walked towards the exit at the end of the night, a bizarre thing happened. I felt something or someone turn me around, but no one was there. To this day I still find this amazing and believe a spiritual presence was there to guide me. Then we were ushered out of the club and I thought I had lost the blonde.

My heart sank, but as I walked out, I heard her cheeky voice shout, 'See you next week.'

I could not get Blondie out of my head. The following week, I turned up at the nightclub again with Adrian, but she was not there. I don't think I took my eyes off the door that night. I had just about given up, but then – in the middle of the dance floor – I saw Blondie. My heart skipped a beat as she came over to say hello.

After I'd eventually established her name – Lorraine – and we'd swapped phone numbers, my world was then significantly challenged when she announced she was married. Nonetheless, we became friends over the ensuing months, and I loved seeing her – even if things were strictly platonic.

In May of 1995, I got a letter from a housing association, offering me a one-bedroom flat. At last, some good news. A couple of weeks later – with loads of support from my family – I moved into my new abode.

Although I still felt isolated, I saved every penny I could – even letting the electricity run out – so I would have enough money for when my kids came to visit, as well as having sufficient to go to Turner's Nightclub. However, I didn't see Lorraine for weeks. Then one day, she turned up but seemed very low. She told me she had split up with her husband and was living in a refuge. I responded by telling her I had a flat and she was welcome to visit anytime she wanted.

Over the next few weeks, we found that we were falling in love, and eventually shared a kiss. Then Lorraine pulled back and left. Confused and hurt, I sat on my little step outside my flat, watching every car that passed, hoping she was returning.

The anticipated 'reunion' did not materialise. I subsequently found out she had gone back to her husband in a last-ditch attempt to make things work. As devastated as I was, I fully understood her need to do the right thing by her kids, the paradox being that although I totally embraced this value, it felt so wrong.

The next day, I was sitting on my settee, feeling like a lovesick puppy, when the doorbell rang. Yes, it was Lorraine. She bounced into my arms and blurted out that she'd tried to make things work, but just couldn't do it any more. Now the only part of my life missing was my kids.

Shortly afterwards, I moved in with Lorraine. We started to gel as a family and managed to get some voluntary work at the Greenway Centre in Sneinton, Nottingham. Although the work wasn't rewarding money-wise, it was definitely powerful to know that we were serving the community and people less fortunate than ourselves. Slowly but surely, I got my confidence and self-respect back. My identity as a strong but sensitive and caring family man was beginning to emerge again. Prosperity is usually associated with people's financial wealth, but for me, this couldn't be further from the truth. The love and security we shared as a family – spanning nearly two decades – was absolutely priceless.

In 1999, Lorraine and I were blessed with a beautiful daughter of our own, Julia, and life seemed idyllic. I then had the confidence to start my own business repairing and selling computers, and prosperity started to present financial rewards. Money felt abundant, and was supplemented by Lorraine getting a job with the local council and progressing along nicely.

However, after nearly two decades, I became aware that things between us were changing. I felt we had no common purpose any more and I found myself asking a lot of questions once again about my identity. This time, though, it was different. I intuitively knew that I was capable of being so much more in my life. For the first time in ages, it was no longer about Lorraine or the family; it was about me and the realisation that a new phase of my life was unfolding like a butterfly emerging from a chrysalis.

Early in 2017, Lorraine confirmed what I already knew – it was over between us. The pain of this crushing news was alleviated somewhat by the fact I agreed we had drifted apart and become totally different people. For weeks after, I found myself in a crazy world of emotional chaos. All the certainty I had ever known had now vanished; I was running on 'emotional fumes', and there were times when I didn't know if I had the strength to survive the moment, let alone the day. I kept sliding into victim mode, and if it hadn't been for the continuous interventions of my loving family and friends – including Paul Lowe – I would not be here to recall the journey of my life.

After working through my recent pain and suffering, I'm now embracing my emerging identity as a warrior who will use my rich life experiences to continue to grow and – more importantly – pass on the lessons I've learnt for the benefit of others.

WOW

It's better to be a loving warrior
than a lonely worrier.

Always play full-out in life -
no half measures!

PaulLowe**HEARTS**

From Dream To Queen

LYN SMITH
(UK and Spain)

I spent most of my life in England, but currently live in Spain. As a teenager, I was subjected to several traumatic experiences that went on to impact my ability to trust, love and enjoy relationships with men for many years.

My personal history is a harrowing one. I didn't have a close relationship with my parents; as kids, we were taught to be 'seen and not heard'. They were strict disciplinarians and didn't spare the rod when it came to corporal punishment.

They always fought a lot. I remember one time when I was about thirteen years old, my dad sent me to run after my mother to tell her to come back because she'd stormed out after yet another major argument.

When I caught up with her, she said through her own pain and anger, 'Go away, I wish you had never been born!' I've never forgotten these words which shook me to the core, negatively impacting my future image of myself. I believed that if my own mother didn't love me, how could anyone else? How could I love myself?

WOW

Take responsibility for loving yourself first.

Throughout my teens, I experienced several sexually traumatic events that no girl should ever have to go through. I was raped at the age of fifteen by a man I trusted at my local swimming club. I was a virgin and naïve enough to think that he'd offered me a lift home out of kindness. That lift cost me the rest of my childhood, a potential competitive swimming career, my education, some good friendships as well as my femininity and dignity. It left me feeling violated, ashamed and dirty. So I didn't tell a soul until I was forty-two. I tried to pretend it had never happened, and for a while it worked.

Then at the age of eighteen, just when I was starting to trust men again, I was drugged and raped by a friend of my then boyfriend. I remember vividly how helpless and vulnerable I felt, and to compound it all, shortly afterwards my mum left my dad.

In her absence, my dad in his pain and despair tried to take advantage and molest me. Fortunately, I was able to escape from his clutches before yet another potentially serious sexual assault took place.

WOW

You always have a choice and a voice. Use them.

This event sent me over the edge and I distinctly remember as a result planning my own suicide. It would have been easy for me to do, as at the time I was working as a Veterinary Nurse and lived in accommodation above the surgery. I had access to the poisons cupboard and recall going as far as reaching for a drug used to immobilise horses which I knew would be fatal to me.

However, something within me stopped that happening. I believe it was the thought of leaving behind my younger brother who was distraught at my parents' separation and was already trying to cope at the age of sixteen with an absent mother and my dad's aggressive mood swings.

WOW

Determination to survive adversity is
your greatest strength.

At the age of nineteen, I joined the Police Force. Upon reflection, I feel this was motivated by the thought that if I couldn't get justice for myself, then maybe I could contribute to getting justice for others. Sadly it proved to be the reverse and I witnessed many guilty offenders getting off with little or no punishment. I left after five years' service, and thereafter began following my passion in various careers in education, coaching and training.

In the seventies, children in the UK didn't have resources like Childline to turn to for help. So I suffered in silence for twenty-seven years before plucking up the courage to start my healing and personal development journey. In 2002, I rang an agency that supports people who have been raped. After an initial assessment consultation, I was told that I 'looked like a typical rape victim'. The counsellor then pointed out – after lengthy questioning – that I was overweight and this was because I was subconsciously trying to protect myself and make myself unattractive to men. Although it sounded harsh, on reflection I know she was right.

Weight-wise, I've yo-yoed up and down the scales all my adult life. I wore black shapeless clothes and didn't wear make-up or nail varnish (and still don't). I didn't wear perfume or jewellery (and have only done so minimally in recent years) – talk about a stereotype! And I know I'm not alone and many people can – and will – relate.

WOW

Always trust and listen to your inner-self.

Then came the devastating body blow. The counsellor ended the consultation by saying, 'Sorry, there is a waiting list. It'll be twelve to eighteen months before a counsellor will become available.' Not what I wanted to hear after feeling I was finally ready to talk.

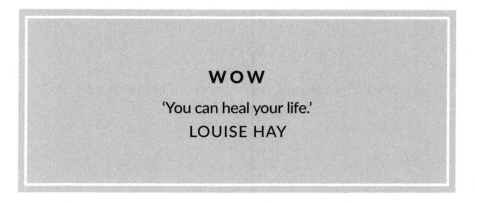

WOW

'You can heal your life.'
LOUISE HAY

Hopefully things have now positively progressed in the UK and worldwide.

Needless to say, all these experiences had a negative impact on my intimate relationships. I remember having a promiscuous phase prior to meeting my ex-husband. I desperately wanted love and to feel lovable, and made the mistake – as do many girls – of using sex to get this need met. Then I went from not caring about my welfare and feeling totally needy and out of control (which only resulted in more hurt and distrust of men) to unconsciously looking for a man (my ex-husband) who would offer me protection, safety, love, stability, and also let me take total control of the relationship.

I got my wish. For the twenty-three years that I was with my ex-husband, I was very controlling. I acted as if I was superior to him, forced my opinion over his, told him how to do things that he was perfectly capable of doing himself, and altered the things he did so they were done my way. I also wore an invisible suit of armour and was, for the most part, a confused, frigid bitch.

WOW

If you're confused, don't worry – a breakthrough won't be far away.

All this was driven by my unconscious need to look after and protect myself on the back of not trusting men. What I ended up with was a man I managed to emasculate on a regular basis. After years of inadvertently changing him to become a male version of myself, I wondered why I didn't find him as attractive any more. It was because I was the dominant one wearing the trousers.

I subsequently divorced this perfectly good man, not because I wasn't happy, but because I felt there was something missing. I felt he had lost his balls, but it was me who had all but castrated him. There was no passion, and although there was love and intimacy in the main, we had a 'friendship' type of relationship. The thing I didn't realise at the time was that this was mostly my own fault – a response to my controlling masculine behaviour.

WOW

Be aware when you're not being your true self.

If you can relate to any of the above, then here's the good news. In 2005 I felt compelled to go on two specific journeys. My first was to address my health. I attended regular group exercise classes and worked consecutively with two brilliant personal trainers at the gym. It took me five years to lose 5 stone (70lbs/32kg) which built up from two half-hour sessions to an obsessive twelve hours per week, yet still I plateaued even though I felt I hadn't reached my ideal target weight. However, I knew I looked and felt really good (despite sometimes looking in the mirror and seeing my old fat self).

My second journey was to seek out the world's leading personal development and relationship experts to heal myself, find out all their secrets and see how they matched with my own years of experiential learning. I immersed myself in gaining knowledge about the differences between how men and women think, feel and behave in regard to their personal relationships. Along the way I discovered some powerful passion and intimacy techniques, strategies and skills that really work.

These techniques showed me how to heal and love myself. Whereas before (with my ex) there was distance, little connection and the feeling of settling for an 'OK' partnership, I have now reclaimed my authentic feminine self. I've learned to let go of control, and trust without feeling the need to protect myself in my invisible suit of masculine armour. I have a relationship full of passion, intimacy and massive connection, where I feel alive, loved and cherished above and beyond my wildest dreams. Finally, I've realised what I've been craving all my adult life. I wanted to attract a strong alpha-male who would treat me like a queen, protect and take care of me, take the lead in a healthy relationship, show me passion, and melt me with his very presence.

Wow! On 3 Jan 2010, I certainly attracted that when I met my soulmate, Paul. So was it all sweetness and light?

WOW

Knowledge isn't power; taking action is.

Unfortunately, no – at least not to start with. Despite having a very passionate relationship with lots of deep love, intimacy and connection, every three to four weeks we'd end up having big arguments. I couldn't understand why. After having had such a calm relationship with my ex (most likely because he wanted to keep the peace), I knew it must be Paul's fault, right?

Wrong!

Believe it or not, it took me over three years of (sometimes very painful) experiences to grasp that the issue of resolving conflicts has a specific sequence and order. I just needed to learn to handle it in a feminine rather than a masculine way.

WOW

Challenge is an opportunity to learn and grow.

To create calm and intimacy where otherwise there would have been conflict and arguments, I learned that I need to diffuse the situation. For example, if Paul gets irritated or frustrated over something and unfairly takes it out on me (I call this 'lighting the fire'), the temptation is for me to react by:

- Getting aggressive (retaliating in anger)
- Becoming defensive (saying, 'Yes, but...')
- Justifying (with my 'I'm right' opinion)

Either way, all Paul feels at this point is another male energy challenging his masculinity. I used to do all of the above on a regular basis, always with the same result. We'd end up having a full-blown argument. We both used to say hurtful things, and Paul would then withdraw to his 'cave', sometimes for days at a time, while I would feel utterly distraught.

I knew I needed to implement some of the techniques which taught me to respond to him in a feminine way and see my vulnerability as a source of strength (not weakness) to pour water on the fire. One simple way I do this is by letting him see that he has hurt my feelings with either his words or his body language. I'll respond, for example, by using my forefingers to point playfully at my bottom lip, which I'll stick out in a little girl pout, complete with sad puppy-dog eyes (just one of many 'feminine' responses I use). He'll instantly feel guilty for hurting the woman he loves and give himself a far harder time about it than I ever could. The result is that the fire has been put out and intimacy has been maintained. I can then pick my moment to have my say on the situation in a calm, feminine way.

I'm really excited to say that since I've been putting the fire out, peace and calm have prevailed.

WOW

Just because you had a bad past doesn't mean
the present or future must be that way.

I know Paul adores me, and we both now make a conscious effort to deal with potential conflicts in a playful, fun or calm way. What a relief! I have personally known what it's like to suffer the trauma of rape and abuse as a young teenager in an era when children weren't encouraged to have a voice. I believe I survived these experiences for a reason – to prepare me to inspire women to know they can have a safer, brighter, more fulfilling future when it comes to their intimate relationships. I specifically help women reclaim their authentic feminine selves in this area.

I feel lucky to have the ultimate soulmate relationship. Paul and I have a healthy, deep love, passion and intimacy with peace and calm, and if we can, you can too.

If you're a woman in a relationship, perhaps you've said or thought these words:

I love my man, but...

- I still feel unfulfilled
- We are more like friends than lovers
- The relationship is lacking passion and intimacy
- The spark has gone
- We argue all the time
- I need more peace and calm in the relationship
- He's distant most of the time

Or if you're a single woman, perhaps you have said or thought these words:

I want a relationship, but...

- There are no good guys out there
- I always attract losers or players
- I never get a second date
- I don't know where to start
- Men don't like powerful/successful women

- I can't trust men
- I seem to push men away

Or whatever else your 'but' is. Do you want to know how to reclaim your feminine power, create/attract your soulmate relationship and feel fulfilled, fully awakened and alive? Then I'm here. I'm genuinely dedicated to helping as many women as possible have the kind of relationship they deserve and for which I'm so grateful. I want to share my discoveries and secrets with you.

WOW

Reclaim your feminine power;
it belongs to you.

I honestly believe these powerful skills will have a positive impact in reducing divorce, domestic violence and suicide.

I have a proven track-record as a Relationship Transformation Expert and International Speaker, based upon my own vast personal research, experiential learning and trainings with the world's leading industry experts.

Understanding the polarisation of masculine and feminine energy resulted in me creating massive attraction and a passionate intimate relationship, feeling alive, fulfilled and at peace. This inspired me to design and present my own course programmes to share these breakthrough relationship techniques with women across the globe. My extensive experience includes coaching women from diverse backgrounds – regardless of their sexual orientation – both nationally and internationally, creating lasting love, passion, intimacy, fulfilment and peace in their personal relationships. I make a difference by helping them make a difference, with a vision of contributing on a global scale.

I would love to be involved in leaving a lasting legacy of safety, dignity and opportunity for children and women who have survived rape, abuse and severe trauma as a result of war crimes and sex trafficking, through the setting-up of worldwide 'you can heal your life' centres/ retreats. With the help of people like you, I know I can do it.

If you want to enjoy a full, intimate relationship at its highest level, contact me, Lyn Smith – The Queen of HEARTS, at www.Hearts-Entwined.com

WOW

Everything will be well in the end. If it isn't at
the moment, it hasn't ended yet.

Feel the power of love
with **HEARTS**Entwined

PaulLowe**HEARTS**

PART THREE

Your Path To Prosperity

Putting
Your House
In Order

Thank you, the reader, for taking the time to invest in this book. I'd also like to thank the global co-authors who have had the compassion to revisit their respective life stories in the hope that you will take something positive from them. As a result, you may want to embark upon a continuous improvement journey that will ultimately enable you to give more – both to yourself and others.

It's interesting how the co-authors – to varying degrees – have used words like pain, learning, loving, and legacy. In reflecting back on the past decades and how I have come to make sense of all the pain, confusion and suffering I've experienced, I have constructed The HEARTS House. This is a concept that embraces all the key considerations that contribute to people feeling like they reside in a good space; one that provides a solid foundation for the belief and confidence to meet all the challenges the external world has to offer.

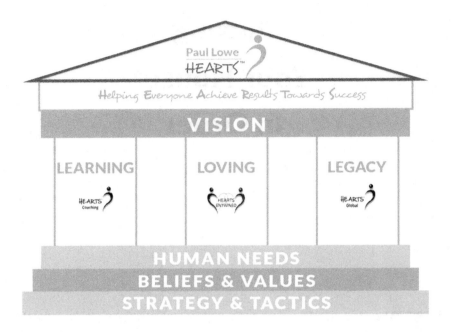

From a structure built on solid foundations, you have the necessary insights to design your own house reflecting the wonderful uniqueness of you. As an example of how to fill the house, I have 'furnished' one with my own influences, starting at the top with my identity.

Identity: Paul Lowe – The HEARTS & Minds Mentor.

Mission: to create and deliver innovative, inspirational, awareness-raising educational projects for individuals, enterprises and communities globally through our HEARTS.

Vision: to achieve my mission by giving people the tools of transformation through world-class coaching, mentoring and training, contributing towards a legacy of a world that inspires everyone.

Human needs: as human beings, we all have needs that must – and will – be met. We will do almost anything to have our needs met. Experience has taught me the power of the Six Human Needs (Robbins): certainty, uncertainty, significance, love and connection, growth and, ultimately, contribution

Beliefs. Our beliefs become our thoughts, which in turn become our words, actions, and then our reality. I believe my purpose on this earth is to contribute. I accept that all the lessons learnt along the way can be passed on for the benefit of others

Values:

- **C**ontribution – making a difference to myself and the world
- **A**wareness – learning to live in the here-and-now
- **R**elationships – harmony by being ACE
  (authentic, congruent and empathic)
- **E**mpowerment through inspired coaching,
  mentoring and training
- **S**uccess fuelled by Learning, Loving and Legacy

Strategy: the 'Three Pillars of Life' approach (Learning | Loving | Legacy) – embracing the journey from pain to prosperity

Tactics: to transform people's lives from pain to prosperity by delivering life-changing messages and programmes, supported by the 'Seven Key Pieces For Your Life's Jigsaw' and the '3A's Approach: Awareness | Accountability | Action'. In relation to Tactics, the 'Seven Key Pieces For Your Life's Jigsaw' was the first of these two vital considerations that contributed towards the progression in my life and creating a secure 'house'.

What kind of house do you want to create?

Seven Key Pieces
For Your
Life's Jigsaw

1. Pain. In August 1968, all my certainty for love and security began to evaporate. I was to replace this with the demon drink as my certainty, temporarily numbing my pain and suffering.

Many people can relate to this. Perhaps a deep-rooted cause is holding them back. Perhaps they are focusing more on the challenge than creating a solution, using a substitute solution such as an addiction, over-eating or infidelity to escape.

Just as pain can be good for us in the short-term by instigating change, it is equally important to be aware of how it can have significant knock-on effects to our lives if we allow it to linger and manifest itself into long-term suffering. For example, many people when they are in pain perceive lots of other areas of their lives in the same negative, distorted way. Fear is given free rein to run amok and create havoc. It's like looking through sunglasses – everything is always dark.

So why am I talking to you about pain? Because I want to enable everyone to let go of it and live a peaceful, loving, fulfilling life. The pain I'm referring to is not necessarily physical, but the mental and emotional pain we carry around with us as baggage.

Why do we carry this baggage of suffering around with us? It's not our fault; most of the time we're not consciously aware that we do it, but it can negatively impact the quality of our life massively.

Where does the pain come from? In the wider world it can come from a sense of loss or lack at the hands of natural disasters, such as an earthquake, flood or famine, or man-made disasters through wars, etc. Closer to home, it usually comes from the life areas of health, career and relationships. It's not the pain itself that is the problem, though – pain is inevitable. It helps us to learn, change and grow. Long-term suffering, however, is optional.

By suffering, I mean negatively reacting to pain, for example self-medicating ourselves by indulging in addictive behaviours such as wallowing in self-pity (playing the victim), abusing food, alcohol, drugs, gambling, self-harming, acts of attention-seeking, aggression, violence, etc. As human beings, we are inherently driven by the need to avoid pain versus the desire to experience pleasure. The vast majority of people take whatever action is needed to avoid pain by papering over the cracks rather than tackling the real issue at the root cause. Consequently, we need to deal with the original challenge at source, delve into the 'C-drive' of our mind and change the program completely. It is no use simply applying white correction fluid to our metaphoric computer screen.

Upon reflection, one thing I know to be absolutely true is that our beliefs can either make us or break us. We can choose to hang on to old disempowering beliefs, or change them to new empowering ones and live a life full of love and fulfilment.

2. Change. My suicide attempt on Saturday 23 March 1974 was very real. It was not a conscious cry for help, but rather a stark realisation that I felt there was no realistic alternative to this hell on earth that I was experiencing. However, the resilience of the human spirit can never be underestimated, and although I was only thirteen, as I held the gleaming razor blade to my left wrist, I had the presence of mind not to end my life.

Because my own world lacked any purpose or identity – other than chaos and devastation – I had built an external fantasy replacement and become emotionally attached to Nottingham Forest Football Club, and their world was crumbling.

Many people can relate to needing this outside distraction – letting someone or something else be responsible and have the power to affect their own happiness. They will never control their own destiny; instead, victimhood becomes their best friend. For example, I have lost count of the number of conversations I've had with women who feel 'worthless' once their kids have grown up and flown the nest, believing their lives are over now that their role as a mother has been fulfilled. In reality, they are so much more than that.

Have you ever made a life-changing decision out of sheer desperation that would prove to make a significant difference to the bigger picture, even if it was only initially intended to offer temporary respite? This was certainly my experience. My newfound decision to fight rather than flee would prove to have profound consequences. This was my first step to leaving victimhood behind; I needed to learn a new way of being.

Most people will do more to move away from the pain of their current situation than they will to move towards the pleasure of an inspirational goal.

3. Learning. In September 1991 – some seventeen-and-a-half years after that fateful decision not to end my life – the demon drink again played a significant part in shaping my future, this time offering a long-term positive outcome on the back of a short-term challenging situation.

I had lost a lucrative job due to a drink-related incident and found myself with limited options. However, the universe provided me with a strong urge to go to University and expand my mind, resulting in me achieving amazing growth.

Spending over ten years on the 'academic wheel' achieving a Teaching and Master's Degree, I learnt immeasurable lessons of a more practical and spiritual nature – I was learning to discover my true life's purpose. While the academic process can prove to be a useful vehicle for stretching our minds, the real power lies in overcoming limiting beliefs such as 'poor working-class people don't go to university'.

Many people know they have so much more to give, but feel frustrated because they don't know what that is or where to start. They strongly feel the need to move away from the pain in their lives, but lack inspiration. Maybe their intimate relationships or careers have now become stale and lack passion; perhaps they're looking to establish their true self and life's purpose but don't know how.

There are often negative connotations associated with learning – usually anchored to our school days – so why not embrace learning as a voyage of discovery? Be passionate or curious about a new way of being and living.

So why do we need to learn? Human beings need to feel like they are growing and contributing or else they'll fail to thrive. Any challenge is an opportunity to learn lessons; there is never any failure, only feedback from which we can grow and progress.

Have you ever noticed that you're repeatedly getting the same life lesson? Ask yourself, 'Why is this happening? What is the learning that I need to take from this event?'

Other than academia, I also spent a lot of time engaging in creative writing – having work published that offered reflections around life, the demon drink, faith and love. Maybe creativity is an untapped area of your life that needs to be explored?

4. Love. In October 2010, the HEARTS brand – Helping Everyone Achieve Results Towards Success – was formed. For someone who had spent his whole life contributing to others less fortunate, I saw this as a natural progression path. However, this motive masked a deeper-rooted one. As I reflect back now, although I was contributing at a high level, I was actually satisfying my own ego-driven need for significance first. While on the surface of it thousands of others benefitted so there shouldn't have been a problem, the reality was I didn't enjoy the journey. I was chasing external results without being internally congruent with my true higher self.

What I didn't have awareness of at the time is that love starts with the self first – not in an egotistical way, but rather from a place of self-forgiveness and self-gratitude. How can we give love if we haven't got a 'love bank' to draw from? If our inner-world is in complete turmoil, we'll look for external validation in all our relationships. We need to take responsibility for creating self-love, forgiveness and gratitude first. How we treat ourselves sets the standard for how others will treat us.

During my poetry phase, I created poems entitled 'The Way Of Life' and 'My Love For You'. Below, I have taken bits from each to create 'Life And Love' reflecting my own thoughts about love.

Throughout life's journey, many different challenges emerge which, at the time, you may not enjoy or even understand – like famine, prejudice and war – but you must rest assured, they are a vital part of life's learning.

Love is the all-powerful emotion that waters us through the aridity of life's desert. It is the difference between merely existing or living life to the full. Life and love are gifts, and like all gifts, they should be treasured.

Love is like the sun – radiating warmth and happiness; and like the wind – we cannot see it, merely feel its power. It is a gift so precious and warm; a gift so blessed, it gives us the faith and strength to carry on.

But I know I cannot give what I do not have, so I invest in my own emotional bank first and save up enough to be able to give to others, so that they feel inspired to do the same.

Although the power of love comes from within, it is awesome to feel loved within a mutually-beneficial, secure and trusting relationship. I will be eternally grateful to the people who have given me love and support over the years.

5. Forgiveness. It's impossible to create self-love while self-hate resides. Liken it to rubbish in a filing cabinet – there is no room for good information to be stored. Love only thrives in the gift of the present, not in yesterday's hurts and pains.

Have you ever heard the saying 'If you don't like your life's story, then change the script'? We can do that by changing a few words, some paragraphs, pages or even the whole book if necessary. So what's in a word? Everything. Because a simple eleven-letter word like forgiveness acts as an umbrella for so many other powerful words, like acceptance, awareness, deservedness and letting go, the last being part and parcel of forgiveness.

Why so? Because before we can move on from any parts of our past lives that are not serving us, we must accept that it's OK to have made mistakes – we are human and this is all part of the learning and growing process. We must forgive ourselves and let go of any guilt.

Forgive yourself if you've ever clung to the past; you are totally powerless to change it. Give yourself permission to let go of the pain from the past, but not the lessons learnt. Letting go is not about being weak; it's about being strong enough to stop being a victim of what happened yesterday, living in the here-and-now rather than being strangled by any fear of what may happen in the future.

I know from personal experience that one of the most natural reactions as a human being to someone hurting us is the desire for revenge. This didn't do anything for me; instead, I spent many years crippled by fear and resentment. I was a prisoner in my own mind. My psychological dependency on alcohol created toxic knock-on effects in almost every other area of my life. What I now know is to deal with the root cause of the problem and then let it go.

As with love, we cannot forgive others until we have truly come to terms with forgiving ourselves first. Once again, this is not about being weak – it is simply about taking full responsibility for and control of our own lives.

So how do we do this? A simple technique to start with is to look in the mirror and tell the person we see how much we love and forgive them. Offer thanks for that beautiful soul being in our life. This may feel uncomfortable at first, but with practice it becomes easier.

With forgiveness and gratitude, there is often an academic debate about which one comes first. My answer is simple. It's not an exact science – consciously focus first on the one that serves you best at that moment in time.

6. Gratitude. What is gratitude – what does it mean? From my own past perspective, it was all about having an appreciation for things that were going my way, so long as I was getting what I wanted on my terms. However, what I now know is that gratitude is a choice for all of us, either lifting our hearts and making us grateful for all the beauty and power of the here-and-now – living in the moment – or making us resentful victims of our past challenging experiences.

Even in the depths of my despair, I somehow had the awareness to know there was something beyond my own plight. I made sense of my pain by being grateful for the chance to fight for others, even when I wasn't addressing my own issues.

Take a moment to enjoy listening to the birds sing, smelling the scent of flowers, feeling the wondrous textures of nature in all her guises, or marvelling at the miracle of a new life entering the world. Most people take these 'basic' things for granted, fuelled by thoughts that they just happen anyway.

Gratitude helps us to put things into perspective and raises our awareness of how special we actually are. It helps to uncover our success – something that is already within us anyway – and truly enjoy the moment.

The benefits of practising gratitude on a daily basis are nearly endless. By doing so, we experience more positive emotions, exude a more confident energy, feel happier and more alive, sleep more soundly and express more compassion and kindness. Gratitude doesn't need to be felt and expressed only at significant events such as the safe delivery of a child; we can be thankful for something as simple as the air that we breathe. Expressing three to five different reasons to be grateful on a daily basis has been proven to increase our well-being significantly.

If we get excited about the benefits of gratitude, it gives us the inspiration we need to make positive changes. One of the best ways to get into the habit of expressing gratitude is to compile a daily gratitude journal/diary. Schedule it as though you're booking an appointment for yourself, choosing your ideal time of day. For instance, if you tend to be exhausted at night, schedule your gratitude slot for the morning instead. Of course, the goal isn't to have a notebook full of declarations of gratitude, but rather to make gratitude a default feeling. By writing down positive things that happen, we become better at recognising the good in our lives.

Gratitude is not some fancy notion that can be picked up and put down whenever it's convenient; it is both an attitude and a practice. It just takes a few moments each day, focusing upon things we are truly thankful for.

7. Prosperity. This really is at the heart of our lives, and was certainly the final piece in my jigsaw, giving me the awareness to live a life full of love, happiness and fulfilment. So what is prosperity? Of the many available definitions, the one I embrace the most is:

> *Prosperity is the state of flourishing, thriving, good fortune or successful social status. Prosperity often encompasses wealth but also includes other factors which can be independent of wealth to varying degrees, such as happiness and health.*

WIKIPEDIA, 2017

As I reflect upon the compilation of my seven-piece jigsaw, I understand how it has provided a model that – although it is not an exact science – offers a realistic framework for each and every one of us to progress and live life to the full.

As well as the multitude of unsung heroes who have contributed to the prosperity of my life, I am extremely grateful to the inspirational teachings of several eminent practitioners.

Pain: Dr Deepak Chopra (2000, p.7) gives insights into how we have it within us to be free from disease and never feel pain. He elaborates to clarify that this is known as 'perfect health'.

Change: Jim Britt (2015, p.6) sets the scene around the change process by highlighting a key question: 'What am I hanging on to from the past that's keeping me from being all I can be now?'

Learning: Tony Robbins (2001, p.45–50) focuses on how beliefs have the power to create, and equally, the power to destroy. It's a question of learning to choose beliefs that serve and empower us.

Love: Catherine Ponder (2006, p.215) talks about loving the self first and how we cannot radiate this all-powerful emotion outwardly until we love ourselves from within. After all, we cannot give what we don't have.

Forgiveness: Louise Hay (2006, p. 7–8) offers that 'to release the past, we must be willing to forgive' – ourselves and others. Taking this a stage further, she then alludes to the fact it's about letting go, not condoning behaviour.

Gratitude: Oprah Winfrey (2014) rationalises being grateful and how the time when we feel least thankful is the time we're most in need of what gratitude can give us. It can transform any situation from negative to positive.

My intention for the jigsaw is that it inspires you to want to piece together your life and create your own beautiful picture – one that is totally bespoke to you then acts as an inspiration to others.

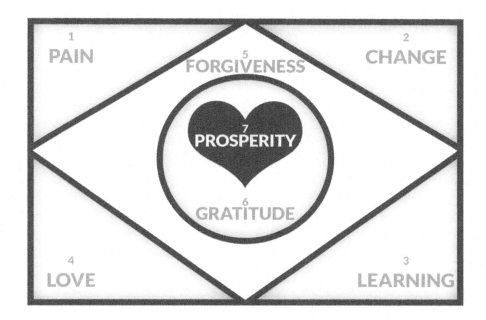

Are you ready to embark upon a voyage of discovery that will unravel your own puzzle and create a beautiful life picture? If so, be curious and committed enough to ask, 'How?' The 3A's approach gives further insights.

The 3A's Approach

The world is littered with self-help advice, tips and general insights into how to fix our lives. I challenge this 'treating people like patients' approach – no one needs fixing. Rather we benefit from a step-by-step empowering journey, one that actually serves us – we don't serve it.

Awareness and desire are the key levers that need to be strong enough to facilitate a change of attitudes, beliefs and emotions. We can't alter what we're not aware of.

Accountability in the form of an experienced mentor is a worthwhile tool to add to our arsenal, guiding us through our many challenges in a positive and effective way while supporting us in reaching our full potential.

Action. We can have access to the best knowledge and support strategies available, but these will never replace the need for us to take action. Our desire to change needs to be strong enough to sustain a voyage of growth and progression that will undoubtedly involve many challenges and exciting discoveries.

As I contemplate my own arduous adventure, I know one thing for sure: I now dwell in a place of happiness, fulfilment and love. This greatly inspired me and the compassionate co-authors in this book to pass on our many positive outcomes, gained from our respective painful lessons. My only caveat on this is the price that's been paid for lessons 'funded' by decades of deep emotional suffering. For many years, I fumbled my way through the dark before coming to realise that the more I cut corners, the more I'd go round in circles.

You don't have to pay that price.

WOW

Take one small step forward each day.
Remember, it only takes a few simple seeds to
grow a densely populated forest.

Want to master the game of life?
Reach out – I can help

PaulLoweHEARTS

For more insights and to share your inspirational
story in a future *Speaking From Our HEARTS* book,
visit: www.PaulLoweHEARTS.com/author

REFERENCES

Britt, J. and Lutes, J. (2015), *The Change (9): Insights into Self-Empowerment*.
    California: The Change

Chopra, D. (2000), *Perfect Health*. New York: Three Rivers Press

Cunningham, K. (2017), Keys To The Vault: 'Falling For The Cause'. Accessed
    17 August 2017 <online at: https://keystothevault.com/falling-for-
    the-cause>

Hay, L. (2006), *You Can Heal Your Life*. London: Hay House UK Ltd

Longfield, A. (2017), Children's Commissioner for England,
    'The Children's Commissioner's Report on measuring the
    number of vulnerable children'. Accessed 14 August 2017
    <online at: https://www.childrenscommissioner.gov.uk>

Ponder, C. (2006), *The Dynamic Laws of Prosperity*. California:
    DeVorss & Company

Robbins, A. (2001), *Notes From A Friend*. London: Simon & Schuster UK Ltd

Wikipedia (2017), The Free Encyclopaedia. Accessed 20 August 2017
    <online at: https://en.wikipedia.org/wiki/Prosperity

Winfrey, O. (2014), *What I Know For Sure*. 'Being grateful isn't easy'.
    Accessed 29 August 2017 <online at: http://www.dailymail.co.uk/
    home/you/article-2743896/Being-grateful-isnt-easy-Inspirational-
    insights-Oprahs-new-book.html>

Winfrey, O. (2017), 'Makers Moments: Realizing Her Legacy'.
    Accessed 20 August 2017 <online at:
    https://www.makers.com/moments/realizing-her-legacy>

Speaking From Our HEARTS Is Proud To Support HEARTS Global Community Interest Company (CIC)

When we read that there are nearly 50,000 children in gangs, you could be forgiven for thinking that we were living in Dickensian England, not the 21st century. Yet they are among hundreds of thousands of children who are vulnerable or living in high-risk family situations.

**ANNE LONGFIELD OBE,
CHILDREN'S COMMISSIONER, 2017**

For example, there are more than 15,000 children with parents who have alcohol issues and almost 12,000 with parents being treated for drug problems. Children's Commissioner Anne Longfield OBE described the figures as 'shocking and very significant', adding that they were 'just the tip of the iceberg'. So it's easy to imagine that these figures would go into the millions worldwide.

All profits from the sale of *Speaking From Our HEARTS* Amazon Kindle e-books are being donated to HEARTS Global CIC, an organisation dedicated to making a powerful, positive difference to communities locally, nationally and globally. This is achieved in two ways. Firstly, by providing a range of business-related services that add outstanding value to individuals and communities; secondly, by re-investing profits back into educational life-improving projects around the globe.

The CIC's predecessor, the Sporting HEARTS charity, provided a sporting chance in life to young people from disadvantaged communities within the UK. Since its formation in 2010, it has positively affected the lives of over 3,000 young people over a six-year period.

We share Archbishop Desmond Tutu's message: 'It is our moral obligation to give every child the best education possible' and recognise that we can all give something, whether that is our time, resources or cash.

We are truly grateful for any donation and would be delighted to talk to you about the difference your gift will make.

To donate to HEARTS Global, please go to:
http://www.heartsglobal.org

ACKNOWLEDGEMENTS

I offer my sincere gratitude to the contributors who have significantly influenced the content of this book.

Firstly, to life itself for giving me the opportunity to learn, grow and serve, no matter how painful the lessons along the way have been.

Also, to the amazing co-authors who had the selfless courage to share their stories in the hope that their invaluable learnings may be passed on.

Next, to Lyn Smith – The Queen of HEARTS – for her patience, passion and unswerving support. She continues to be a vital sounding board in all that I do.

But most of all to you, the reader, for investing in yourself by purchasing this book.

ABOUT THE AUTHOR

Paul was born on 25 October 1960 in inner-city Nottingham, England. As an only child, he was influenced in his formative years by the love of his mother and grandmother.

Despite his humble existence, Paul was happy. However, from the age of eight, for over four decades, his life became a stark polarisation of darkness and light.

It was during the decade of concentrated education that Paul became conscious of his personal development journey. A degree in Education was then followed by a Master's degree in Customer Service and Quality Management, the latter strongly influenced by eminent practitioners such as Dr Stephen Covey, Dr W. Edwards Deming and Tom Peters.

Paul is a qualified ILM level-5 Business Coach, New Insights VIP Life Coach and Robbins Strategic Intervention Coach. He now uses his diverse experiences to make a positive impact on the lives of individuals and communities globally.

As the founder of the PaulLoweHEARTS brand, he is committed to our HEARTS:

Helping Everyone Achieve Results Towards Success.